The child at risk

MANCHESTER
1824

Manchester University Press

The child at risk

*Paedophiles, media responses
and public opinion*

Anneke Meyer

Manchester University Press
Manchester and New York

distributed exclusively in the USA by Palgrave

The right of Anneke Meyer to be identified as the author of this work has been
asserted by her in accordance with the Copyright, Designs and Patents Act 1988.

Published by Manchester University Press
Oxford Road, Manchester M13 9NR, UK
and Room 400, 175 Fifth Avenue, New York, NY 10010, USA
www.manchesteruniversitypress.co.uk

Distributed exclusively in the USA by
Palgrave, 175 Fifth Avenue, New York,
NY 10010, USA

Distributed exclusively in Canada by
UBC Press, University of British Columbia, 2029 West Mall,
Vancouver, BC, Canada V6T 1Z2

British Library Cataloguing-in-Publication Data
A catalogue record for this book is available from the British Library

Library of Congress Cataloging-in-Publication Data applied for

ISBN   0 7190 7344 8 hardback
EAN   9780 7190 7344 1

First published 2007

16 15 14 13 12 11 10 09 08 07   10 9 8 7 6 5 4 3 2 1

Typeset in Sabon 10/12 pt by
by Servis Filmsetting Ltd, Manchester
Printed in Great Britain
by CPI, Bath

Contents

List of illustrations

List of abbreviations and note on the text

Quotations have been extracted from newspaper articles and focus group discussions. In all quotations **bold** type shows emphases added by the book's author to highlight certain discourses, while *italicised* type represents original emphases. Double full stops are used in focus group quotations to indicate a brief pause or hesitation.

Acknowledgements

This book could not have been completed without the help and support of many people over the last few years. I am particularly indebted to all those who gave up their time to participate in focus groups, and whose opinions have become central to my research and this book.

As many of the ideas reproduced here emerged through my PhD thesis I wish to thank my supervisor, Beverley Skeggs, for her guidance and infinite enthusiasm. My colleagues at the Department of Sociology at Durham University have all been very supportive, but my special thanks go to Paul Johnson and Steph Lawler, who have read drafts and provided useful feedback, and become good friends.

Ich muss mich auch besonders bei meiner Familie bedanken, die mich immer und in jeder Hinsicht unterstuetzt hat. Sowohl meine Eltern, Carmen und Claus Meyer, als auch meine vielen Geschwister, Martin, Swanni, Merle, Leane und Lukas.

Last but not least I owe very special thanks to all my friends for sustaining me throughout the solitary experience of writing. Without them I would have never finished this book (and remained sane). Among them, I have to single out Elaine Brick for some unforgettable times in Newcastle, Hannah Stewart and Marc Whalley for always keeping my spirits up, and Tony Brady for his constant love.

1

Introduction: history, frameworks and research

Paedophilia: a social problem

Police have warned paedophiles in the North not to travel to countries hit by the tsunami disaster because of fears they might target orphaned children. Convicted sex offenders got letters detailing the ban last week. The action comes in the wake of sickening reports of child-snatch gangs and perverts preying on the vulnerable youngsters in countries such as Indonesia. A spokeswoman for Northumbria Police, which has 750 people on the Sex Offenders' Register in the force area, said: 'We actively manage sex offenders in the Northumbria force area and that includes preventative measures to stop further offences at home and abroad.' John Gee, spokesman for Christian Aid, praised the move. He said: 'This is a responsible action by the police. Paedophiles are the last people on earth that we would want to have going to the tsunami disaster area and we are very happy that Northumbria Police are being so pro-active and doing their job properly.' (P. Doherty and C. Smith, 'Child sex perverts get tsunami warning', *Sunday Sun*, 27 February 2005)

This excerpt from one of my local newspapers indicates that paedophiles are currently a high-profile problem in the UK. In the wake of the tsunami disaster in South East Asia in December 2004 the British public made significant charity donations, the government promised financial aid, and several local police forces banned convicted child sex offenders from travelling to the affected region, purely as a precaution. This episode illustrates many of the themes and arguments running through this book.

Paedophilia is not a 'natural' problem but a socially constructed one, i.e. the ways in which paedophilia and paedophiles are understood, constructed and responded to are thoroughly social. This is not a radical claim. Much social research – whether anthropological (e.g. Douglas 1992), sociological (e.g. Cohen 1972) or literary (e.g. Kincaid 1998) in perspective – has suggested that there is an abundance of risks, threats, dangers and issues, and that society selects and constructs only *some* of them as its social problems. Paedophilia as a social problem is not fixed or inevitable. It is not high up on the agenda because of any inherent features such as paedophiles being evil, or paedophilia being particularly horrific, or a threat of huge proportions. Rather, these 'natural', essentialist explanations are the very products of social constructions and discourses. For instance, paedophiles are currently one of the most demonised and othered groups in society; they are constructed and understood as so thoroughly evil and despicable that not even liberals or Christians want to speak up on their behalf. As the Christian Aid spokesperson put it, they are 'the last people on earth' that we would want. These constructions of paedophiles as evil persons and a large-scale problem make it possible for the police to think of travel bans for child sex offenders in the absence of any real incidents. Police actions also confirm the very constructions which facilitate them, reproducing paedophiles as a major social problem.

While it is hardly radical today to assert that social problems like binge drinking or yob culture are socially constructed, paedophilia and child sexual abuse are different. It remains difficult to apply the social constructionist perspective publicly because child sexual abuse, as Davis (2005) has argued, has become the paradigm case of victimisation. Marked by a collective narrative around extreme gravity of experience, violation and damaging consequences, child sexual abuse appears as the most 'natural' of social problems. Moreover, the social constructionist approach disrupts common moralistic interpretations. These conceive of interest and concern as 'natural' and moral because interest in paedophilia and fervent condemnation of paedophiles are equated with caring for children, with fighting on behalf of those who cannot fight for themselves. The social problem approach exposes this easy moralism not only as mistaken but as hypocritical, concealing 'true' motivations and foreclosing the enquiry into motivations. Paedophilia, as a social problem, is not inherently more horrific or pressing than other social problems, and social reactions privileging it through persisting interest and emotiveness can therefore not be explained through moral concern with the wellbeing of children. Any outrage and repulsion is also combined with fascination. Paedophile stories sell; they are often detailed, appear as front-page news and become the subject of media campaigns. Yet interest and fascination are erratic. South East Asia, especially Thailand, has long been a holiday destination popular with Western males looking for underage sex (O'Connell Davidson 1995, 1998), but this topic remains mostly low-profile and these men are often not classed as paedophiles. This enables the *Sunday Sun*, as other papers, to represent post-tsunami events and measures as novel, as directed at a sudden problem.

Fascinations and the erratic nature of interest suggest that society's reactions to paedophilia are not motivated by the problem itself, which persists, or simply by altruistic concern. My aim is to dispel the easy moralism and sanctimonious equations which suffuse debates around paedophilia, and to this end the subject of this book is *how* and *why* paedophilia is produced as a significant social problem. The book explores the mechanisms and reasons for society responding with such interest, emotion and indignation. The terms 'paedophilia' and 'paedophiles' are difficult to distinguish in their exact meanings today as they have come to be used interchangeably. Put simply, paedophilia refers to a condition, 'thing' or practice, while paedophile(s) refers to individual(s). When it is conceptualised as a social problem we would expect paedophilia to become the term encapsulating and referring to it, but this has not been the case. Today people tend to talk about paedo*philes* as the problem, an indication that a social problem is conceptualised through individuals. This conceptualisation has arguably become predominant with the terminological shift from child sexual abuse to paedophilia (Kitzinger 1999). Here, I will refer to paedophilia and child sexual abuse as much as possible to avoid individualised understanding. This is, however, a book about common forms of understanding, discourses and meanings. Hence referring to the 'paedophile problem' or simply 'paedophiles' as the shorthand will often be unavoidable and indicative of the ways in which paedophilia is often understood by the wider public, the media and others.

This book is an enquiry into the discourses through which we construct and understand paedophilia, and how forms of understanding are linked to attitudes, opinions and practices. It is a book about meanings and not, as many others are (e.g. Silverman and Wilson 2002; Taylor and Quayle 2003), about policies.

Consequently, it does not aim to suggest or improve measures for dealing with paedophiles but to unravel and scrutinise our discursive understanding of paedophilia, which forms the very basis of social and penal policies. This entails establishing whether we are concerned about paedophiles, why we are concerned, and how our views, practices and feelings are linked to the discourses through which we understand and construct paedophilia. The slightly elusive 'we', or 'society', is – if necessarily inadequately – captured by empirical research into the opinions and practices of parts of the media (newspapers), recent governments, and some members of the public who participated in focus groups. All these major social agencies suggest that since the 1990s paedophilia has become a very sensitive and public topic capable of raising great emotions and levels of interest in the UK. Paedophiles are widely seen to pose a significant threat to children which has to be talked about and tackled.

As far as the media are concerned, quantitative studies (e.g. Silverman and Wilson 2002; Critcher 2003) have shown that since the 1990s the number of paedophilia-related stories has risen dramatically and remained at a very high level generally. Within this time frame there have been certain periods where coverage and interest have peaked, these peaks being usually linked to and driven by particular events (e.g. the Dutroux scandal in Belgium in 1996, the murder of Sarah Payne in summer 2000 or the murder of Holly Wells and Jessica Chapman in summer 2002). This alludes to paedophilia controversies possessing a global dimension, both in the sense of high-profile cases eliciting emotive reactions in countries other than the UK (e.g. Belgium, Ireland, the US, Canada and Australia) (Critcher 2003) and in the sense of an increasing focus on the Internet turning paedophiles into a global threat. The high-profile case of Toby Studabaker (e.g. Wainwright and al Yafai 15 July 2003), a US citizen who travelled to the UK to meet a 12-year-old British girl he had communicated with on the Internet, is a case in hand. Yet the UK represents the focus of this book.

Arguably, it is the intensity as well as amount of media coverage which indicates a major social problem. A number of newspapers including the *Sunday Express* in 1997, the Scottish *Daily Record* in 1997 and most famously the *News of the World (NOTW)* in 2000 have run campaigns to out paedophiles by publishing their names, addresses and photographs (Critcher 2000a; Kitzinger 1999). The *NOTW* used its 'name and shame' campaign to demand legal changes, namely the introduction of indeterminate sentences and public access to the sex offender register (also known as community notification). There is no newspaper today which will argue that paedophiles do not pose a significant problem, or which will speak up on their behalf. Paedophiles have become a group of people who are universally despised and feared.

While many studies on media interest and coverage focus on the news, interest in paedophilia has spilt over into media products other than news, both fictional and non-fictional. Kitzinger (1999) has pointed out how paedophilia as a topic featured in many documentaries, series and soap operas in the 1990s. This trend has continued as paedophiles have become a popular topic in many UK non-news programmes. To name but a few examples: paedophiles and paedophilia are a frequent topic of discussion on radio talk shows (e.g. Radio Five Live, 17 December 2001 and 9 May 2004) and talked about on television chat shows, entertainment shows and magazine programmes such as *This Morning* (e.g. 5 December 2002, ITV on Internet paedophiles), *Loose Women* (e.g. 8 August 2003, ITV on the dangers of paedophiles on the beach) or *Richard and Judy* (e.g. 15 November 2003, Channel 4, on Internet paedophiles). Paedophilia as a topic has featured in soaps such as *The Bill* (e.g. in February 2003 numerous episodes concentrated on paedophile abductions, ITV) or *Merseybeat* (e.g. 19 January 2004, BBC1), and has been the central subject of one-off dramas, for instance *Real Men* (12 and 13 March 2003, BBC2, on paedophile rings in child-care homes). Moreover, many documentaries and documentary series have been broadcast on paedophilia, e.g. *The Hunt for Britain's Paedophiles* (June 2002, BBC2, following the work of Scotland Yard's Paedophile Unit), *Police Protecting Children* (March 2004, BBC2, on police work in relation to so-called 'predatory paedophiles'), *The Protectors* (May 2004, BBC1, on risk management and the release of paedophiles), *Cutting Edge: Child Sex Trade* (9 October 2003, Channel 4, following UK paedophiles relocating to Romania), or *Flesh and the Devil* (15 January 2004, Channel 4, on 'paedophile priests'). This suggests that paedophilia as a social problem and topic is no longer confined to politics and news but preoccupies various forms of media and saturates our culture.

Government and legal interest match the concern of the media with paedophilia. Since the 1990s successive governments have

introduced a number of legal measures in order to combat paedophiles; for example, the sex offender register created in 1997 cen-
trally lists all those cautioned and convicted of sex offences (Cobley
2000; Thomas 2000). The Criminal Justice Act 1991 has allowed
for the attachment of additional requirements to the probation
orders of sex offenders, and since 1995 the release of sex offenders
with life sentences has been made dependent on extra licence conditions. Since the Crime and Disorder Act 1998 sex offenders can
be subjected to extended supervision after release (Thomas 2000).
All these measures create more punitive conditions as they restrict
the possibilities of release and lives after release. The law has also
become more punitive in terms of sentences; since the 1980s, sex
offenders have been subject to harsher sentences as reflected in an
average increase in the length of imprisonment of convicted offenders (Sampson 1994; West 1996). This development has partly been
enabled by the Criminal Justice Act 1991 and the Crime Sentences
Act 1997, under which 'dangerous offenders', defined as sexual or
violent offenders, can receive longer custodial sentences and will
automatically gain a life sentence if convicted twice of a serious
offence. These changes mean that the legal system has *additional*
control measures available for dealing with sex offenders, ranging
from longer custodial sentences and extended periods of supervision
after release to special conditions and requirements being attached
to release (Cobley 2000).

This punitive trend continues, as reflected in the Sexual Offences
Act 2003. Representing an overhaul of British sex crime laws, it has
created a new offence of 'grooming' children for sexual abuse and
automatically classifies sexual intercourse with a girl under 13 as
rape. Another bill proposed by the Home Secretary in May 2003 has
suggested the creation of a new 'life means life' sentence for multiple murders of adults and children, and for single murders of children involving sexual conduct or abduction (Travis 8 May 2003).
Specifications of abduction and sexuality strongly suggest that this
new law is aimed at paedophiles and the subjection of 'violent paedophiles' to indeterminate sentences. Therefore there has recently
been much activity on the part of the government and the legal
system concerning paedophiles. All the measures taken, from the
creation of new laws and sentencing guidelines to the implementation of sentences and release conditions, are increasingly punitive
and repressive. The government has also set up the Scotland Yard

Paedophile Unit in the 1990s and launched an advert campaign against the dangers of paedophiles on the Internet in January 2003. Governmental and legal measures are responses to media actions as well as constructive of paedophilia as a social problem – the police issuing convicted child sex offenders with travel bans exemplifies this active role.

As far as the general public is concerned paedophilia can generate great emotions. It is a topic heatedly debated in public places such as pubs and on TV shows, and there have been public protests and vigilante actions (e.g. in Portsmouth in 2000 or in Cambridge in 2002), and even vigilante killings of suspected paedophiles, such as Barry Sewell (Clixby 6 May 2005) and Paul Cooper in 2005 (Herbert 23 March 2005), or Arnold Hartley in 2003 (Carter 1 December 2003). While only a small minority engages in such protests and vigilantism, opinion polls have shown generally high levels of concern, interest and outrage among the public. For example, a MORI study in 1998 revealed that parents were concerned about the safety of their children in summer school holidays, and that abduction of a child by a stranger was the single biggest fear (56 per cent). This study represented parents from social classes D and E as consistently the most concerned about the safety of their children (MORI May–June 1998). In polls directly related to paedophile incidents (e.g. the murders of Sarah Payne and of Jessica Chapman and Holly Wells) nearly half (47 per cent) of respondents thought of contemporary society as unsafe for children, and the vast majority (78 per cent) believed contemporary society to be more dangerous for children than in the past (MORI 23 July 2000). Following the killings of Jessica Chapman and Holly Wells, 71 per cent of parents reported an increase in concern about the safety of their children, and 61 per cent said that they were less likely to leave their children unsupervised (MORI 19 September 2002). As these polls were explicitly about the topic of paedophiles they suggest that the dangers and lack of safety parents were concerned with was strongly related to paedophiles.

However, matters are not so clear cut. Opinion polls themselves can be incitements to fear as their performance suggests that there is a serious problem which has to be researched. The discourse of the 'good parent' (Lawler 2000) may prohibit the expression of a lack of concern and worry, leading to high percentages showing fear and confirming paedophiles as a serious problem. The analysis of opinions polls is further complicated by contradictory opinions. There are high levels of worry about the safety of children, especially in relation to paedophiles. Yet when asked about measures for improving the safety of children the top two measures named spontaneously in numerous polls were 'more policing' and 'better parenting' (MORI 23 July 2000, 20 August 2000, 11 December 2001, 16 December 2001). The targeting of paedophiles is also seen as a safety measure but it is at the bottom of the list, with 2–3 per cent mentioning it (MORI 23 July 2000, 20 August 2000). In a MORI poll from 16 December 2001 respondents wanted to improve child safety through a number of specific anti-paedophile measures such as electronic tagging of paedophiles (3 per cent), public naming of paedophiles (5 per cent) and tougher sentences for child attackers (6 per cent). But other polls (e.g. MORI 11 December 2001) did not include any suggestions on specific anti-paedophile measures. These statistics are ambiguous. It is significant that if asked about general safety measures, respondents mention specific anti-paedophile measures – no other criminal group is directly named in these statistics. However, as many of these polls are about paedophiles, respondents might be encouraged to think of even general questions in terms of paedophiles. Moreover, the numbers of individuals putting forward these ideas are comparatively small, as the majority relies on traditional and general measures such as increased policing.

Opinion polls also demonstrate popular demands for tough punishments of paedophiles. For example, one poll showed that 58 per cent of respondents wanted to reintroduce the death penalty for child murder, and 30 per cent for serious sexual abuse of a child; 75 per cent agreed that those committing serious sexual crimes against children should be imprisoned for life (MORI 23 July 2000). Polls and figures suggest that respondents are worried about the safety of children. They consider paedophiles a significant threat which deserves harsh forms of punishment. However, these views are slightly incongruent with the opinion that the safety of children is best ensured through the introduction of general protective measures rather than specific anti-paedophile measures.

The limits of moral panic theory

Social problems are culturally and historically specific. Paedophilia has not always been a social problem; before the 1970s the term 'paedophile' was confined to academic medical circles, while nowadays it has become a household word (Cobley 2000; Jenkins 1992). Before the 1970s the media and the public were largely unconcerned with paedophiles, even though there were images of the 'pederast' as the lone, male and rather pathetic child molester. Pro-paedophile arguments were even published in magazines such as *Achilles Heel*. Paedophiles were 'discovered' by the media and the wider public in the 1970s when paedophilia was linked to the problematisation of child pornography and homosexuality. Since the 1980s paedophiles have been connected to rings and networks, sexual violence and murder, with the effect of becoming highly organised and violent figures (Jenkins 1992, 1998). In the late 1980s the Cleveland Affair (Campbell 1988) put child sexual abuse firmly on the social agenda, as a social problem tied to the family. Following much controversy there has arguably been a conceptual shift since the 1990s away from child sexual abuse as a problem *of* the family to a problem *outside* the family (e.g. Corby 2000; Kitzinger 1999). Since then 'the paedophile', as the stranger figure embodying the danger of child sexual abuse, has become the focus of attention. This figure of 'the paedophile' continues to be seen as highly dangerous, organised and violent, and the Internet has recently given such ideas new impetus as it is understood as multiplying the opportunities for paedophile abuse (Jenkins 1998). This raises the fundamental question as to why paedophiles are constructed as a major social problem now.

This book's exploration of this question is grounded in a critique of moral panic theory, which has informed much social scientific work on paedophilia. According to Cohen (1972) the condition of moral panic refers to deviant behaviour, which has been present for some time, attracting sudden attention and eventually censorship. This arguably happens at times when normative boundaries are blurred and in need of clarification. The model suggests that a moral panic is present when a form of behaviour is labelled deviant and subjected to the following nine processes: exaggeration/distortion, prediction, symbolisation, creation of an orientation paradigm, creation of images, emergence of causation models, sensitisation, intervention of the control culture and emergence of an exploitative culture. The media play a key role in instigating and sustaining moral panics as they systematically manufacture fear and create a folk devil, an entirely negative figure. Other moral entrepreneurs and the control culture are seen as quickly joining in the moralising

and behaving as if what the media said was true, thereby crystallis-
ing media messages into more formal opinions and finalising the creation of a folk devil. For the public this arguably has a confirmative
effect. The net result of these processes is deviance amplification,
which manifests itself in the widespread view that the form of
deviance is a major problem which something needs to be done
about. This results in the control culture taking measures to combat
the problem, and subsequently in a decline of the moral panic as
interest and fear wane. The episode is termed moral panic because
it is characterised by extensive moralising and the reaction is considered disproportionate to the objective threat posed.

Paedophilia has been claimed as a classic moral panic topic by
those working within this theoretical framework (Critcher 2003;
Jenkins 1992, 1998), and it does fit Cohen's processual model in
many respects. Paedophiles have been extensively stereotyped, the
threat of stranger danger has been exaggerated and 'the paedophile'
has become one of the most terrifying folk devils of recent times.
However, there are other aspects which do not fit the model; for
example, paedophiles have proved to be a durable issue. Describing
social reactions as disproportionate panics, because of the assumption that the threat is largely imaginary, is problematic: it is pre-
sumptive, generalised and judgemental, and relies on contentious
notions of the objectivity and measurability of risk. While being
useful as a heuristic tool, the moral panic approach is severely
limited in its analytic and explanatory potential. It relies on totalistic, media-led explanations as the media are seen to manufacture
fear and the 'panic' reaction of society is read off from the media.
This simply assumes consensus in reactions and the reaction itself,
panic, and conceives both the media and society as single, mono-
lithic organisms. As a consequence the questions *why* and *how*
paedophiles come to generate such interest and concern can simply
not be answered, unless one accepts the media as an overarching
explanation.

Contemporary theorists working within the moral panic framework have approached this explanatory deficit by turning to risk
theory, in its sociological form. They use the concept of risk society
not to explain single cases and their dynamics but to account for the
social predisposition to panic, for the public mood that the media
are seen to capture and exploit. Following Beck (1992), this is
seen to happen by way of risk society producing heightened risk

consciousness and a proliferation of manufactured uncertainties, which in turn create feelings of insecurity and anxiety. These conditions are existentially troubling and conducive to seeing all kinds of 'normal' things as risky, and to buying into media-manufactured fears. The social atmosphere in late modernity is characterised by a general state of anxiety, which is conducive to panics and expresses itself in a variety of specific fears and issues, paedophiles being just one of them (Critcher 2000b; Furedi 1997). These ideas are appealing and intuitive but there are significant problems with them.

First, this general, totalistic take on risk society presumes a lot and empirically demonstrates little (e.g. we do not know if people really panic), and as such it fits the moral panic view of society as a total organism experiencing fear. Empirical evidence for assumptions is rare and difficult to produce on such a grand level, especially if the aim is to establish historical comparisons such as *shifts* in opinion or consciousness.

Second, only half of Beck's argument is adopted. Beck (1992) suggests (a) that risk society generates uncertainty, and (b) that uncertainty generates self-reflexivity in order to combat uncertainty. While the first part of this logical chain has been adopted (risk produces uncertainty), the latter part (uncertainty produces self-reflexivity) has been ignored. Self-reflexivity refers to individual or social engagement with an issue which includes confronting one's own involvement and adjusting one's actions in the light of these assessments. Thus self-reflexivity is a conscious, cognitive, reflective and hyper-rational attempt to deal with risk and does not sit well with the reactions moral panic theorists see as arising from the condition of risk society: automatic, irrational panics and fears. Adopting only part of a theory and ignoring aspects which do not fit one's own model is clearly problematic.

Third, the assumption that risk and uncertainty create insecurity and anxiety, which are existentially troubling and create fear, is difficult. Both Beck (1992) and Giddens (1990, 1991) employ only a residual psychology, and it is by no means certain that living with risk and anxiety is a necessarily or totally negative experience. Kincaid (1998), for example, believes that anxieties contain elements of pleasure and desire as well as fear, and that to an extent we seek to stimulate our anxieties. Moreover, it is unclear why uncertainty, risk and ambiguity are seen as necessarily producing anxiety and fear when many theorists, including Beck, take into account the liberating aspects of late modern conditions of ambiguity, flux and instability. These issues are serious because risk and moral panic theorists put significant theoretical weight on the links between risk, anxiety and fear (Goldblatt 1996).

Fourth, if late modernity is a risk society marked by manufactured uncertainties, then this prompts the question of how these largely non-personal risks (ecological, economic etc.) are translated into 'panics' about human relations, such as paedophilia. Why does society not panic about unemployment or the greenhouse effect? Anxiety displacement is often offered as the explanation (e.g. Furedi 1997; Hollway and Jefferson 1997; Ungar 2001), but it is too neat and convenient, and leaves open the central question as to why society should avoid facing its 'real' problems.

Fifth, moral panic theorists use risk theory in a way which means that risk only comes in to explain the preconditions of social reactions and not the reaction itself. The reaction is still read off from media analyses and explained through a 'media creating panics' paradigm, meaning that specific reasons and dynamics in the generation of concern remain again undiscovered. It is not revealed why one subject rather than another should become the focus of emotions and interest at a particular time. The explanatory deficit of moral panic theory remains unresolved because another grand theory is simply brought in as a supplement.

Theoretically, this book moves beyond this supplementary and totalistic framework through alternative frameworks of discourse, risk/reflexivity and neo-liberal governance. In contrast to moral panic approaches it is grounded in empirical research extending beyond the media to include the wider public and the government and its law enforcement agencies.

Objectives and research

This book's objective of understanding social concern with paedophilia necessitates identifying prevailing images, discourses and beliefs surrounding paedophilia, as well as who is concerned and to what extent. In short, research needs to unravel the dynamics generating and shaping concern. The combination of media and focus group research has become popular in audience research, offering the possibility of investigating how audiences relate to and make sense of specific media texts and contents (Hansen 1998). The approach of this research is broader, based on the assumption that discourses enable, structure and shape particular forms of understanding and knowing issues around paedophilia. The media might be able to impact on popular and official understanding through the deployment and exclusion of certain discourses (Mills 2003). A research design incorporating three qualitative methods (discourse analysis, focus groups and documentary research) *explores* rather than *assumes*, and *explains* as well as *describes* the opinions, understandings and reactions of the media, the wider public and the government and its law enforcement agencies.

Focus group research[1]

The opinions and reactions of the wider public towards paedophiles have been largely ignored by academic research. Opinion polls conducted by MORI with members of the public have shown high levels of concern with paedophiles, but also that people are often very 'reasonable' in their assessments of the scale of the problem. The reasons behind concern and its 'contradictions' have not been established as this is beyond the power of survey methods (Hansen 1998). Focus groups are a suitable method for achieving such insights into the *how* and *why* of people's reactions and attitudes. As a qualitative method, focus groups focus on meanings and interpretations, which are crucial to understanding the dynamics, complexities and ambiguities of human attitudes. The dialogic, interactive nature of focus groups encourages the recognition, articulation and defence of beliefs and opinions, offering insights into the factors shaping them. Moreover, comparative and contrastive aspects facilitate the establishment of a range of experiences, opinions and reactions (Frey and Fontana 1993; Morgan and Krueger 1993).

The focus group study comprised three groups of 7–10 participants each and openly centred on 'popular attitudes to paedophilia' as the research topic. Groups were set up as semi-structured discussions around five general and open-ended questions (e.g. 'What do you think about paedophiles?') designed to give participants space to explore particular issues they considered important, and to cover the major issues which had emerged from the media analysis carried out previously. In terms of sampling the systematic random rule did

---

1 See appendix for further details on individual focus group participants.

not apply (Bloor et al. 2001), and two of the groups were pre-existing while one was formed purely for the purpose of the research. Social class was used as the major break variable for practical reasons, to encourage open debate, and for theoretical reasons, as social class was envisaged as a factor structuring attitudes (Hansen 1998; Knodel 1993). Roughly speaking, the three groups covered three social classes, the middle class, upper working class and lower working class. Hence, not all social classes were represented, and the group of upper-working-class students occupied an aspiring rather than established class position with a strong possibility of upward social mobility (see below). Unintentionally, gender also became a homogeneity factor as 23 out of 27 participants were female. Non-parents and males were underrepresented due to access points such as nurseries and Sure Start centres being predominantly used by parents and females, and due to a lack of positive responses from potential male participants. Overall focus groups were not representative of the whole population, in terms of either numbers or composition, but focus groups do not have to consist of statistically representative samples because generalisation is not their prime objective (Bloor et al. 2001).

The first group consisted of seven participants: Amy, Kerry, Abi, James, Miles, Jack and Ravi. All of them were at the time completing an access course at Manchester College of Arts and Technology, with the intention of progressing on to an undergraduate degree in education. On the basis of the Registrar-General's social class classification they could be broadly classed as upper-working-class (Crompton 1998). Kerry, Abi and Miles had children. Newspaper readership was considerably mixed as most participants indicated that they frequently read a range of newspapers including local papers, national tabloids and broadsheets.

The second group consisted of ten participants: Pilar, Hannah, Kate, Emily, Ellie, Vic, Christine, Helen, Celia and Rachel. All participants were female and had children. This group was not pre-existing but mixed participants with various university affiliations, such as mature students, university teaching staff and university administrative staff. As a result social class homogeneity was not achieved. On the basis of the Registrar-General's social class classification a slight majority of participants could be described as middle-class (Pilar, Hannah, Ellie, Helen, Celia and Rachel), and the remaining four participants (Kate, Emily, Vic and Christine) as working-class. Middle-class participants clearly dominated the discussion so that the data produced mainly bear the mark of their attitudes. Their views as well as newspaper affiliations, such as the *Guardian*, the *Observer* and the *Independent*, further marked them out as middle-class and broadly liberal in political outlook.

The third group consisted of ten participants: Sinead, Lisa, Donna, Pat, Beth, Dorothy, Tanya, Claire, Sarah and Fiona. This was a pre-existing parent group at Trinity House in Rusholme, Manchester. As a community centre affiliated to the government's Sure Start programme, Trinity House provides childcare facilities, workshops and discussion groups for parents. Except for the group leader, Fiona, all participants could be broadly described as lower-working-class according to the Registrar-General's scheme. This classification was also reflected in housing and newspaper readership, which focused on a variety of national tabloids and included some local papers (Tunstall 1996).

Media research

The media are central to the construction and understanding of paedophilia because they disseminate information to the public and provide a forum for debate. Further, they actively construct public debates through their discourses, interpretations and images. This media analysis focused on the *NOTW* and the *Guardian* because the *NOTW* continues to play a prominent role in the construction of paedophilia as a social problem, e.g. through the 'name and shame' campaign in summer 2000, and in conjunction with the *Guardian* this meant the analysis captured opposite ends of the newspaper spectrum, the *NOTW* being a conservative tabloid and the *Guardian* a liberal broadsheet.

Discourse analysis was used in order to establish the major discourses through which paedophilia is understood and constructed in the media. Critical discourse analysis (CDA) (Fairclough 1995, 2003) relates discourses to discursive practices (production, distribution and consumption) and wider social practices. Through these three dimensions discourse analysis connects the linguistic and wider social dimensions of the paedophilia controversy, and avoids treating the media as a separate entity. Media coverage of paedophilia is related to political, legal and social practices, and these practices are also discursive practices as individuals consume and (re)produce media discourses in their conversations and interactions. Therefore CDA offers a theoretical framework for analysing the media and linking different levels of research.

For the purpose of discourse analysis a discourse is a unit of meaning beyond a single sentence, i.e. it emerges from several sentences, repeated words and ideas, and whole texts and images (Fairclough 2003). Discourse analysis of the media concerns the first and core dimension of CDA: a discursive analysis of media texts, texts being understood to refer to both language and images. On a practical level, CDA uses critical linguistics for analysing language texts, and social semiotics for analysing images (Schroeder 2002). Critical linguistics as a tool for analysing media language is indebted to Halliday's functional grammar and social semiotics (e.g. Fowler 1985), and postulates that language has an ideological function. Ideology and discourses are different concepts but they can be reconciled in the sense that discourses can have ideological effects, i.e. they contribute to relations of power. These effects can be unravelled by putting CDA of texts into a larger social analysis context which considers the impact of discourses on power relations (Fairclough 2003).

According to critical linguistics, ideology and discourses work through lexical and syntactic processes and choices, such as terminology, modality, syntactic transformations etc. (Fowler 1985). This necessitates identifying constructions of discourses and ideologies through these choices and processes, as well as semantic relations such as collocations, i.e. patterns of co-occurrence of words or metaphors (Fairclough 2003). All these aspects are useful for a media discourse analysis. The examination of lexical and syntactic features can reveal *what* discourses are circulated around paedophilia (e.g. perversion), *how* these features are used to construct discourses (e.g. through lexical items such as 'pervert'), and *what* and *how* certain discursive subject positions are created for the reader. For example, the discourse of perversion constructs paedophiles as perverted and opposed to the 'normal' sexuality of the majority, the latter being the discursive position set up for the audience to embrace. Critical linguistics is useful for identifying discourses but forms only part of CDA; textual analysis can be deepened by exploring attitudes to difference, the exclusion and inclusion of certain voices in the text or the value assumptions being made (Fairclough 2003).

CDA in terms of images draws on an approach developed by Kress and van Leeuwen (1996, 2001), which is variably called social semiotics, discourse semiotics or multi-modal communication. The authors see social semiotics as an adaptation of critical linguistics to image analysis. Images are analysed by looking at the meanings and discourses created through people, objects and places shown (equivalent to lexis) and compositional structures (equivalent to syntax). Linguistic and image analyses are integral aspects of discourse analysis because both modes of communication are involved in the construction of discourses. CDA in this research was applied to a range of newspaper text forms, images and genres related to paedophilia over several years. Within this wide time span the analysis focused on texts from periods of heightened media interest, such July–September 2000 or August 2002, as discourses become most obvious and prevalent in such periods. The wide scope, in terms of time and numbers, is useful as discourses emerge across numerous texts and can change over time. However, the spatial constraints of this book result in a focus on texts rather than images, and while discourses and discursive figures have been identified as emerging over years and across many texts and images, only the most pertinent examples could be included.

Media analysis preceded and informed documentary and focus group research. Documentary research took the form of retrieving legal documents from legal information databases (e.g. Sexual Offences Act 2003 on Lexis Nexis) and academic law books (e.g. Cobley 2000), as well as accessing official documents via the media (e.g. government adverts) and government-initiated websites (e.g. thinkyouknow.co.uk). Analyses of these documents as well as focus group discussions were informed by CDA, in particular the major discourses and discursive figures which it had revealed as central to the media understanding of paedophilia.

Newspaper politics and style

A brief discussion of the styles and politics of the *Guardian* and the *NOTW* is important for contextualising and better understanding their responses to paedophilia. Newspapers are commonly divided into three categories: broadsheets or up-market papers (such as the *Guardian*), mid-market papers, and tabloids or down-market papers (such as the *NOTW*). Categorisation is based on the socio-economic make-up of the newspaper's readership, e.g. more than 80 per cent of a broadsheet's readership typically belongs to social classes A, B or C1, while this figure is around 35 per cent or lower for tabloids. Tabloids and broadsheets are also differentiated by some general stylistic and content features. For instance, tabloids are characterised by large front-page headlines and much of the material carried is visual, i.e. pictures, photographs or big letters. In contrast to this broadsheets are much more densely written and contain roughly three times as many words as tabloids in one edition. Further, tabloids typically contain a relatively low number of non-UK news stories and a high number of light news, entertainment and human interest stories. News stories in tabloids often have a personal angle while broadsheets present themselves as serious news coverers (Jucker 1992; Tunstall 1996). Tabloids and broadsheets further vary in terms of style, both in lexical choices and syntax. Tabloids such as the *NOTW* use language which tends to be more colloquial, informal and sensational. Words are generally simple, often abbreviated, and there is an absence of long, complicated or foreign lexical items. Similarly, the syntax of tabloids tends to be less complex than that of broadsheets; in the latter, sentences on average contain more modifiers, are longer, and more often contain subordinate clauses (Jucker 1992; Simon-Vandenbergen 1986).

In the UK there is a longstanding connection between the press and political parties. Newspapers have a general affinity with a political direction and tend to support one party clearly during elections, even if newspapers are also known to switch party loyalties over time. For instance, the *Guardian* can be broadly classified as a liberal progressive paper with a traditional Labour/Liberal Democrat party affinity. Historically, this has expressed itself in election support for those parties (Seymour-Ure 1977), and since the arrival of New Labour the *Guardian* has consistently supported the Labour Party in the 1997, 2001 and 2005 national elections. In 2005 this support was maintained despite misgivings about the Labour Party's decision to get involved in the war in Iraq (*Guardian* 19 April 1997, 6 June 2001, 3 May 2005).

However, today official party support is no longer simply or deeply indicative of a newspaper's politics. Since the rise of New Labour and its neo-liberal philosophy there has been a shift among newspapers towards the new left of the political spectrum, with the majority of daily newspapers supporting the Labour Party through the last three elections. In the 1997 and 2005 elections the same three newspapers supported the Conservatives: the *Express*, the *Daily Mail* and the *Daily Telegraph*. The Labour Party was supported by five newspapers in 1997 (the *Sun*, the *Daily Mirror*, the *Guardian*, the *Daily Star* and the *Independent*) and by four dailies in 2005 (the *Sun*, the *Daily Mirror*, the *Guardian* and *The Times*). In this last election the *Daily Star* did not officially back any party and the *Independent* switched support to the Liberal Democrats because of their consistent opposition to the war in Iraq. Labour majorities in terms of newspaper party support are a recent development as the British press has traditionally been heavily skewed towards the Conservatives (Seymour-Ure 1977). The Labour Party now enjoys the support of previously Conservative papers such as the *Sun* and *The Times*, while traditional Labour supporters like the *Independent* have switched loyalty to the party which is currently considered to be more left-wing than the Labour Party, the Liberal Democrats. These developments mirror general shifts and disputes within the Labour Party since the inception of New Labour, with left-wing or so-called Old Labour supporters feeling alienated and inadequately represented. In a world where neo-liberalism has become hegemonic (Frank 2001) and the policies of the two major parties have greatly converged and sometimes been 'reversed', it becomes difficult to judge what counts as liberal/conservative, left/right, progressive/traditional. Old dichotomies no longer do full justice to the new world.

Newspapers do not only express their political opinions through official party support during elections; over the years they also tend to give more space to parties they support and take sides in the discussion of party policies (Seymour-Ure 1977). The *Guardian* can roughly be described as a liberal, left-leaning and progressive paper, not so much because of its official Labour Party support but rather because of its day-to-day policy stances. For example, it has been opposed to the war in Iraq (if inconsistently), is concerned about the introduction of ID cards as a threat to civil liberties, rejects detention camps for asylum seeker and believes in the rehabilitation potential of many offenders. However, the task of outlining newspaper politics is further complicated by complex changes in the press/politics relationship. Newspapers may have become increasingly partisan and political as they actively try to shape politics

(Riddell 1998) but at the same time the broadsheets may be becoming politically detached and partisanship less predictable, i.e. newspapers' political views and party affiliations are more changeable. Part and parcel of this process is arguably the decline of the single editorial voice. Previously, it determined a newspaper's stance but contemporary broadsheets allow many diverging voices, which are expressed in various feature articles, opinion columns and analyses. In this context the editorial voice has become one, albeit an important, voice among many. Contemporary newspapers are more committed to certain issues or policies, such as Europe, environmentalism or drugs, and less to political parties. As a consequence party support is changeable and editorial opinion is unstable (Seymour-Ure 1998).

The *NOTW* captures the opposite end of the newspaper spectrum. In contrast to the *Guardian* it is a Sunday tabloid with a traditionally populist, right-wing political stance (Tunstall 1996). Historically, this has expressed itself in support for the Conservative Party during elections. However, in the three elections since 1997 the *NOTW* has backed the Labour Party (Greenslade 1 May 1997; *NOTW* 3 June 2001, 1 May 2005), showing just how crude an indicator official support has become for newspaper politics. The *NOTW* embraces all those Labour policies which the *Guardian* criticises, such as the war in Iraq or ID cards, and on crime and immigration the *NOTW* wants generally more drastic and punitive measures than are currently in place. Therefore on the level of attitudes to particular policies the *NOTW* and the *Guardian* are very different, their support for the same party simply emphasising the Labour Party's ability to appeal to very different groups and the Conservative Party's inability to gain the vote of even its 'natural' supporters. Further, compared to the *Guardian*, the *NOTW*, as a tabloid, devotes little space to politics, let alone policies, and discussions remain necessarily short and basic. Exceptions are campaigns, such as the 'name and shame' campaign or the 'drug tests in schools' campaign. As the demands fuelling campaigns are quite specific some, if simple, details on policy are needed. The *NOTW* is therefore not as political a paper as the *Guardian* and its populism means that any political affiliation is relatively weak and changeable. Similarities and differences in politics between the two papers are one factor shaping their respective responses to paedophilia, especially opinions on legal governance.

Explaining social concern with paedophilia:
alternative frameworks

In addressing the constructions of and reactions to paedophilia this book adopts a broadly Foucauldian approach which focuses on discursive constructions and figures that underlie understanding and are linked to power, control and governance. Paedophilia as a social problem is controlled through the processes of discourse, governance and risk/reflexivity, which result in a contemporary crisis of neo-liberalism and an inability to diminish concerns through increased regulation.

Discourse

Foucault conceived of discourse as a system of sanctioned representations and statements which constructs a topic in a particular way (through clusters of ideas, images, practices), and thereby produces specific, meaningful ways of knowing and talking about it. Thus discourses are about the production of meaning, knowledge and practices, as the former two will necessarily enable and govern our thoughts and actions (Mills 1997). Discourses endow things with meanings and produce our knowledge about them. Discourse is a historical concept in that things mean only in specific historical contexts, and in each period discourses arguably produce very different forms, objects and practices of knowledge. Within one period discourses tend to appear across a range of texts and images – and as forms of conduct – in a number of institutional sites of society.

The knowledge produced through discourses entails certain ways of knowing, the generation of certain objects of knowledge and the production of subjects. All are time- and culture-specific. Foucault suggests that discourses produce subjects in two senses. First, discourses produce figures or subjects who personify particular forms of knowledge, such as 'the madman' or 'the pervert'. Second, discourses produce a position for the subject (reader, viewer etc.) from which its meanings make most sense. We must locate ourselves in these constructed subject positions to make sense and are thereby subjected to discursive meanings, rules and power. Yet there are also various social positions which, in conjunction with subject positions, structure access and positioning to discourse (Hall 1997, 2001).

Discourse, as a form of knowledge, is intimately tied to power but this does not mean that discourses always work in the interest of those in power or that their reproduction is perfect. For Foucault power is a dispersed network which does not work in traditional, hierarchical ways. Every discourse contains the possibility of rejection as a well as acceptance, and there are alternative discourses providing alternative forms of knowledge. These can be mobilised to undermine and criticise dominant discourses, meaning that even though there might be dominant discourses at a particular time, their dominance is never certain. The struggle over the dominance of discourses is precisely the struggle over power – the power to know (Valier 2002).

This theoretical framework informs an approach to the topic in terms of discourses, i.e. identifying and analysing the major discourses, discursive figures, ideas and concepts circulated around paedophilia. These discourses inform and enable ways of understanding and knowing, which shape reactions. Discourses exist in and are expressed and perpetuated through language, images and practices. They are (re)produced, challenged and changed across various sites and agencies. We are all exposed to and actively involved in the production of discourses on paedophilia through a variety of sources and practices, which together form one discursive space. Within the framework of discourses the question of media power is addressed. The media are able to promote or encourage certain ways of understanding issues around paedophilia by circulating and employing particular discourses to the exclusion of others.

Understanding of paedophilia, both in the media and in focus groups, revolves around three key discursive figures: the innocent child, the good parent and 'the paedophile'. The innocent child is an asexual, pure and vulnerable figure, while the good parent is marked by altruism, responsibility and care. 'The paedophile', who comes to embody the social problem of paedophilia, is a complex and detailed figure: evil yet human, cunning and pathological, violent and perverted. These three figures are connected in their constructions and derive meanings from connections. For instance, it is the asexual innocence of the child which renders paedophile sexuality perverted and 'abnormal'. It is the vulnerability and weakness of the child which demand adult protection and construct those who provide this protection – the parents – as good and moral. These three figures are central to our understanding of paedophilia as well as the forms of governance we engage in to combat the problem.

Governance and neo-liberalism

Paedophilia, as a social problem, is governed. Foucault defined government as the 'conduct of conduct', i.e. the more or less calculated means to attempt to shape behaviour and action (Gordon 1991). Government is carried out by a multiplicity of agencies (including the government, the media, businesses etc.), which employ a variety of techniques and forms of knowledge (Dean 1999a). This raises questions such as how paedophiles are controlled and regulated. More specifically it directs enquiry towards the strategies, agencies and institutions involved in the governance of paedophilia, and the forms of knowledge informing governmental practices.

From a Foucauldian perspective government can be directed at the self (techniques of the self) as well as others, at individuals or the population. Government always seeks to shape conduct through the individual and her or his desires, interests and beliefs rather than being a direct imposition on society as a whole (Dean 1999a). The terms 'government' and 'governance' are often used interchangeably and have much in common, but governance can be distinguished from government by being both broader and more specific. It is broader in that its object of enquiry can involve *any* area containing *any* form or attempt of actors exercising control over themselves or others. This is expressed in the definition of governance as 'any strategy, tactic, process, procedure or programme for controlling, regulating, shaping, mastering or exercising authority over others in a nation, organisation or locality' (Rose 1999: 15). In contrast to this, government studies tend to confine themselves to systematic, political forms of control (e.g. Dean 1999a), and see social issues in terms of their impact on political thought and attempts at government (Rose 1999). However, the governance perspective is grounded in sociology and more specific than the government perspective in terms of analytics and questions. It seeks to describe its objects (actors, organisations) in terms of actions and motivations, patterns, rules and structures. The government perspective is not concerned with regularities but informs studies on regimes of truth which make government possible, on the variety of strategies, technologies, ends and/or authorities involved in government (Rose 1999). Here, I use the term 'governance' because paedophilia as a social problem involves practices of governance at many social levels, official and unofficial, state and non-state, systematic and unorganised, such as the government introducing new laws or parents regulating their children's movements.

Governance is moral and normative as it refers to attempts to direct and regulate behaviour of certain social groups to (re)produce society in a particular and good way. The specific contents and strategies for achieving these good ends, as well as the ends themselves, vary with different rationalities of government (political philosophies) and with what counts as popular common sense. Governance is not, strictly speaking, tied to any particular political rationality; however, there is a particular affinity with neo-liberalism. Governance, as compared to government, is often loosely interpreted as a form of regulation which is relatively indirect, weak and reduced; i.e. a form of minimal state regulation and intervention, which neo-liberalism advocates. Further, the two historically coincide in their resurgence. Recent history has witnessed a shift in governance towards neo-liberalism, which refers to a governmental rationality that promises to increase efficiency and competitiveness by extending market rationality to all spheres of life. This market philosophy is wedded to the welfare state and public services, the latter not being destroyed but changed and reduced through 'reforms' and marketisation (Colclough 1991). Neo-liberalism has been taken up in different forms in the UK, the US and France. In the UK neo-liberal forms of governance since the late 1970s have meant a reduction of state intervention, both regulation and provision, in many areas of socio-economic life, e.g. health care, pensions or child care. This development is justified through the supposed efficiency of the market, which is introduced as provider and regulator, and a rhetoric of individual free choice, of individuals as citizens with rights and responsibilities (Dean 1998, 1999b).

Against this backdrop we can hypothesise that paedophilia is not simply another social problem but one which generates a crisis of neo-liberal governance and legitimation by producing disputes between the government, the media and the wider public over the adequacy of official measures for dealing with paedophilia. The governance of paedophilia is marked by extensive state intervention, which exposes the limits and contradictions of neo-liberalism and market rule by showing (a) that the market cannot regulate everything, and (b) that neo-liberals do not always advocate neo-liberal, market-based measures for regulating social issues. The exposition of these contradictions leads to disputes and turns paedophilia into a crisis-generating issue.

Sexuality and governance
Sexuality is a central issue as paedophilia is commonly understood as a deviant form of sexuality. Paedophiles are not just offenders but become a category of people defined by their sexuality, a sexuality constructed as deviating from the norm, which is taken to be heterosexuality focused on adults. Foucault (1978) suggests that sexuality is governed through sexual figures and historically there are four figures that correspond to strategies of the deployment of sexuality: the hysterical woman, the Malthusian couple, the onanistic child and 'the pervert'. All four figures are objects of knowledge and control, and society attempts to govern through them by shaping individual conduct. However, today these figures are arguably outdated and would not work to regulate conduct. For instance, the onanistic child is no longer a prime figure as the focus is on children being sexually abused by adults rather than sexually 'abusing themselves'. 'The pervert' is too generalised as there are numerous and different sexual 'perversions' or 'perverts' that are talked about and fascinate (paedophilia, bestiality, men sexually attracted to large women etc.). Instead, I want to argue, 'the paedophile' has become one of the central new discursive figures and as a much more detailed figure than 'the pervert' it might be easier to know and regulate. Sexual perversion is just one aspect of 'the paedophile', who is also produced through many non-sexual behaviour patterns and mindsets. These aspects provide quite intricate instructions for how to regulate paedophilia.

Applying Foucauldian thought, we can suggest that the paedophile controversy is not only about reproducing 'the paedophile' as the ultimate 'pervert', an object which governmental and scientific authorities try to know and control, but also about fostering and reaffirming 'normal', 'unperverted', 'natural' forms of sexuality and figures. These could be seen as embodied by the Malthusian couple, the heterosexual couple whose sexuality is geared towards procreation; but this is too simplistic and out of date for what is happening in contemporary society. The paedophile controversy arguably means that the category of 'normals' or 'respectables' can become wider, as indicated by developments such as the 2005 civil partnership legislation which allows same-sex couples to formalise their relationships and thereby benefit from legal and financial rights previously reserved for married heterosexual couples (*Guardian* 5 December 2005, p. 8). It can include all adult-centred heterosexuals, whether single or in couples, or it can include all those whose sexuality is centred on adults, whether heterosexual or homosexual. Thus the paedophile controversy both reaffirms and redraws the lines; the ultimate dividing line between 'normal' and 'deviant' sexuality is no longer the gender but the age of the 'subject of desire'. This also means that paedophiles become the focus of control and government. Those who are discovered to have sexual contact with a child are subjected to legal punishment, and science is used to know and understand a sexual orientation towards children with the aim of treating and changing it, for example through sex offender treatment programmes.

Reflexivity and risk

Risk/reflexivity theories are central to paedophilia as a social problem because it is framed as a risk to children which governments and parents should reflexively manage. Moreover, crime control generally has been marked by the spread of risk assessment as a form of governance. This development is linked to neo-liberalism because risk has proliferated as a central feature of neo-liberal governance, despite being politically polyvalent. Risk is a technique of governance to shape human conduct for specific ends. As a technique of neo-liberalism risk has become individualised and privatised, i.e. there is little collective risk management or social insurance, as risk management, prevention and minimisation have become the responsibility of individual actors (Dean 1999b). This governmentalist perspective on risk (e.g. Dean 1998; O'Malley 1996) is strongly constructionist and conceives of risk not as a real, ontological, calculable entity but as a calculative rationality. It is a way of thinking about, representing and ordering reality, a moral and political technology. As a governmental strategy risk is involved in the regulation and monitoring of the population. Through these strategies risks become real, for example risk allows for the intervention and designation of groups of individuals who are high-risk or at risk.

In sociological accounts (Beck 1992, 2000) late modernity or risk society represents the stage of reflexive modernisation, which works through the twin processes of individualisation and detraditionalisation, and generates a new logic of risk distribution. These processes fragment social and employment relations and lead to a proliferation of risks and insecurities. Yet reflexive modernisation also dissolves social structures (economic, political and ideological) and increases freedom as agency is freed from structure. The consequences of reflexive modernisation are ambivalent.

In reflexive modernity risks produce reflexivity, which aims to minimise uncertainty and risk, and informs significant changes in structural organisation and existential experiences. Reflexivity, whether institutional or individual, refers to serious engagement with an issue involving confrontation, monitoring and regulation of the self. It is a way of achieving security, *against* expert systems and science. However, if increased reflexivity is one product of increased risk, another one is increased anxiety. For Beck anxiety represents the paradigmatic experience of life in reflexive modernity. Again, the outcome of risk society is ambivalent, encompassing reflexivity and fear, and the consequences of anxiety are ambiguous, too, including potentially both solidarity and scapegoating of socially weak groups.

Giddens (1990, 1991) defines risk as *presuming* danger; people are at risk when they find themselves in dangerous situations. He shares Beck's core ideas on the centrality and changing nature of risk and reflexivity in late modernity, the developmental stages model and the radicalisation of doubt. Moreover, Beck and Giddens both adopt a weak constructionist position where risks are seen as real but socially and culturally mediated (Lupton 1999). Yet while Beck sees heightened risk consciousness and reflexivity as the result of a proliferation of real risks, Giddens conceptualises the proliferation of risk consciousness as grounded in radical doubt and reflexivity. Thus for Beck risk produces reflexivity, and for Giddens reflexivity produces risk (awareness). Giddens also adopts a more individual emphasis, linking risk to trust and danger, and focusing on the impact of uncertainties on the self, identity and close personal relationships.

Mary Douglas's (1992; Douglas and Wildavsky by 1982) anthropological and cultural take represents the third major perspective on risk. She rejects distinctions between objectivity and subjectivity and the claim of the measurability of risk. Risks are mediated by culture and community, yet real; risk is the 'socially constructed interpretation and response to a "real" danger' (Lupton 1999: 39). Douglas emphasises that notions of risk and danger have merged.

Originally risk was a neutral concept relating to the probabilities of an outcome, but today risk arguably possesses purely negative connotations. There are no 'good risks'; risk has become the equivalent of danger and the two concepts are used interchangeably (Douglas 1992). Douglas' approach further suggests that risk issues are not technical but profoundly political and moral, involving constant value judgements: risk is 'unacceptable danger'. Risks are pervasive in late modernity and the prioritisation and selection of some risks for attention can only be grounded in moral judgements, as risks are immeasurable. Reasons for prioritisation lie, in a functionalist fashion, in individual and societal interests as well as morality. Douglas maintains that risks are selected and constructed to protect moral principles and values which a majority is committed to and has vested interests in. These values are important to social groups to maintain boundaries between their selves and the 'Other'. Used as a political strategy, risk serves to assign blame, responsibility and accountability, and often this blame is directed towards already marginalised 'Others' who transgress moral boundaries (Douglas and Wildavsky 1982). Risk, as the social and cultural reaction towards the breaking of rules and norms, symbolically reflects some real threat to the social system (Douglas 1992).

Conclusions

Alternative theoretical frameworks as well as empirical research form the basis of the following chapters, which cover major themes in the social constructions of and reactions to paedophilia. Chapter 2 explores the discursive constructions of children and childhood as the 'at-risk' group. It argues that in issues and stories around paedophilia children are predominantly understood through a discourse of (asexual) innocence, which in turn is identified as central to the sacred status of the child and the moral outrage provoked. Chapter 3 charts the major discourses and concepts which are circulated around paedophilia, and argues that they amount to the construction of 'the paedophile' as a particular discursive figure. This figure is maintained, in a rather contradictory fashion, in conjunction with universalising claims that anyone could be a paedophile, and the dangerousness of the paedophile figure is located in precisely these contradictions and ambiguities. Chapter 4 moves the focus of enquiry away from 'the paedophile' as a figure and on to paedophilia as quantitative risk, examining media and focus group constructions of the scale of the paedophile threat in real and virtual spaces. It argues that while individuals can challenge media constructions the latter have a power to incite fears, in some people, and shape practices as well as opinions. In the case of the Internet its riskiness is revealed as constructed and understood through specific concepts such as identity play and virtual 'grooming'. Chapter 5 examines how paedophilia is governed, by both the government and parents, and hypothesises that it exposes a crisis of neo-liberal forms of governance as official measures are heavily disputed. Further, the figure of 'the paedophile' is identified as being both ungovernable and easy to govern, resulting in increased legal governance which is nevertheless unable to diminish public concerns.

2

Children and childhood

Children and childhood are central to paedophilia, which is conceived as a risk to children. To say that childhood is a social construction is not to deny any biological dimensions but to emphasise that the meanings of childhood and children vary considerably over time and with cultures. This chapter explores these meanings and the ways in which they shape the understanding of paedophilia. It outlines three major discourses of childhood – evil, innocence and rights – all of which construct children as possessing an essential nature and childhood as being a special stage of life marked by these essential characteristics. Historical analysis reveals discursive shifts from the child as evil being to innocent and rights-bearing being, from the child as a source of economic worth to one of emotional value. The discourse of innocence arguably remains dominant in the understanding of child sexual abuse. This is important as the social reaction to paedophiles can be grounded not just in the sacred status of the child (Zelizer 1985) but in the particular dynamics between sacredness, innocence, asexuality and crime. These dynamics are also analysed to reveal the particular function of a moral rhetoric, as adults justify and legitimate any opinion, attitude and course of action by reference to children.

Discourses around childhood

Many historians agree that prior to the nineteenth century the modern concept of childhood as a special stage did not exist and children were often absent, e.g. from politics or the law. However, there is disagreement as to whether this means that children were thought of as possessing a particular nature or not. For Ariès (1962) children prior to the seventeenth century were simply seen as miniature adults without a particular nature or being. Children were rather obscure, the general attitude towards them was marked by indifference, and their worth was primarily economic as a source of future labour. Childhood in these times was short; once the child had demonstrated some adult capacities such as strength and reason it was incorporated into adult life in the form of work and expected to contribute economically to the family. In terms of moral and sexual attitudes both Ariès (1962) and Foucault (1978) note that adults did not see any need to constrain themselves in front of children. The idea of children's sexual innocence did not exist and children were exposed to all kinds of sexual talk, joking and fondling. Indeed sex seemed to be a primarily physical act lacking the morality associated with it in later ages. However, interpretations of this unconstrained behaviour differ. While Ariès argues that it was grounded in a belief that children were either unaware of or indifferent to sex, Foucault sees this attitude as indicating a recognition of children's sexual awareness.

In contrast to Ariès a number of writers (e.g. Jenks 1996; Valentine 1996) have argued that the lack of a modern concept of childhood as a special stage did not mean a lack of ideas around the nature of children. Prior to the seventeenth century they identify a prevailing discourse of evil, which constructs children as base, self-centred and bearers of sin, as well as easily corrupted. The evil or Dionysian child was a threat to itself and society, and subjected to harsh forms of discipline intended to civilise it and destroy sin. This discourse of evil did not feature in any of the media texts on paedophilia in this study, and focus group participants only used it in debates on false allegations of child sexual abuse. This discourse is not generally unpopular; several writers have noted that it is frequently deployed in understanding crimes committed by children (e.g. Jenks 1996; Valentine 1996), suggesting that its absence is particular to the topic of paedophilia in which the discourse of innocence dominates understanding and debate.

The discourse of innocence, which emerged with Romanticism, sees children as close to nature, inherently virtuous, pure, angelic and innocent. Driven by contempt for the adult world of reason – associated with corruption and vice – Romantics located goodness and morality in children. Childhood became a moral and glorifying concept; the discourse of innocence idolised children and presented them as beings to be worshipped. Moreover, for the first time children were seen as a specific class of persons with specific needs. The discourse of innocence encouraged sentimental and emotional relations with children, and a way of thinking of children in terms of their needs. Children came to be valued for themselves, not as future adults, and were turned into objects of love and affection, i.e. sources of emotional value. As a consequence children became truly irreplaceable. The focus on needs was translated into childrearing practices which were less harsh and built around care and attention. Caring for children's needs concerned mainly their wellbeing and protection. The need for protection arises out of the child's innocence which makes it weak in the sense of being ignorant of and vulnerable to the corruptions of the adult world (Ariès 1962; James et al. 1998; Jenks 1996). Prior to these times parents did have affection for their children but being a good parent was less obsessive, less on display (Lawler 2000), and mixed with economic values.

With the discourse of innocence sexuality and morality became central issues in relation to children. Many sexually charged practices were identified as 'adult vices' and deemed dangerous to children, whose innocence had to be protected from the danger of 'pollution'. Of course sexuality, like innocence, is socially constructed and what counts as 'sexual' or 'sexy' varies over time and across cultures (Kincaid 1998). Childrearing doctrines emerging in eighteenth- and nineteenth-century Europe required children to cover up their bodies, and stipulated that children should not share beds or be left alone with servants. Further, adults were required to moderate their language and manners as children were not to be exposed to sexual talk or activity (Ariès 1962). A contradiction emerges as the purity of children and the absence of adult vice imply that children are asexual or pre-sexual in the sense of lacking adult knowledge, experience and desire for others. But the constant pre-occupation with preventing opportunities for sexual activity or seduction suggests that children do have a sexuality which can be appealed to. This contradiction of denial and regulation, silence and obsession, has been identified by Foucault (1978) as characteristic of the Victorian period. The denial of child sexuality in the discourse of innocence was accompanied by a rising scientific interest in child sexuality as one of the 'other' forms of sexuality, and by a multiplication of discourses on child sexuality. The pedagogisation and sexualisation of children was one of four strategies to regulate sexuality in the eighteenth and nineteenth centuries, and it corresponded to the figure of the masturbating child. All children were seen as prone to engage in sexual activity, and although this universal occurrence suggests 'naturalness', child sexual activity was conceived as contrary to nature and physically and morally dangerous to individuals and society. According to Foucault this resulted in a war against onanism, initiated by medical science and spread to parents, teachers etc., a war which was, however, far too obsessive to aim at extinction (Foucault 1978).

The discourse of innocence

Law and policy

Today the discourse of innocence continues to be powerful, especially as far as the understanding of child sexual abuse and paedophilia is concerned, which is evidenced in legal and political changes from the nineteenth century to the present day. The discourse of innocence constructs children as needing and deserving protection, and the state has come to provide such protection. Early campaigns linked the discourse of innocence with practical issues of labour and education, and thereby introduced views of childhood as incompatible with wage earning and synonymous with schooling, education and dependency. By 1914 these modern views of childhood had arguably been legally, socially, educationally, medically and politically institutionalised (Hendrick 1997). The turn of the twentieth century is particularly important. The spreading acceptance of the discourse of innocence resulted in a desire to provide for children universally and standardise childhood experiences. Children achieved a new social and political identity and policies brought about social transformations. Paid child employment declined as schooling became more universal and further legislation restricted child labour (e.g. Prevention of Cruelty to Children Acts 1889 and 1894). As a consequence the duration of childhood increased immensely and the child became more dependent (Davin 1999; Hendrick 1997).

The power of the protectionist logic and concern with child welfare at the turn of the century can be revealed through legislation on child abuse. Jackson's (1999) study, based on legal records of child sexual abuse cases between 1870 and 1914, shows that child sexual abuse in this period was problematised and reported. Nevertheless, many cases went unrecorded and overall the law was more likely to be involved in cases of extra-familial abuse. Jackson locates the underreporting of incest in three factors: the disgrace and shame this brought on the family, the difficulty of applying the stereotype of the evil abuser to a family member, and the legal circumstances of the period. Sexual intercourse between blood relations was not outlawed until the Punishment of Incest Act in 1908, and wives were unable to give evidence in court against their husbands until the Prevention of Cruelty to Children Act in 1889. This latter act also allowed children to give evidence in court, recognised physical and mental cruelty to children as a legal offence, and allowed the police to arrest those maltreating children and enter homes where children were thought to be in danger. Both acts were landmarks in child legal history, making sexual abuse within the family and parent–child relations generally a matter for the state. Child protection became a duty and right of the state, especially where families were seen to have 'failed' or harmed their children; the state gained the power to condemn, intervene and govern. These legal changes were motivated not only by child protection logic rooted in the discourse of innocence, but also by a widespread preoccupation with incest. In the nineteenth century incest was conceptualised as a problem of the lower social classes and connected to lack of space, dubious proximity and antisocial primitiveness (Foucault 1978). For Foucault the laws, emotions and assertions mobilised in relation to incest (e.g. ideas of a 'universal taboo') represent acts of self-defence against the incestuous implications of the modern family as a deployment of sexuality and centre of sexual incitement.

Jackson's study suggests that child sexual abuse and incest have a long history in terms of occurrence and attracting social attention. They existed as distinct concepts and forms of sexual abuse well before the twentieth century. People were aware of child sexual abuse, and legal measures outlawing it were lagging behind popular opinion, as reflected in wives reporting incest before 1889 and communities dealing with child sex offenders through ostracism and violence. Moreover, the contemporary discourse of evil paedophiles is not new but can be retrieved in legal records of verbal confrontations between offenders and parents of victims (Jackson 1999). While the child sexual abuse debate in contemporary society has arguably reached new levels of intensity, many of its core aspects are historically rooted.

The post-Second World War period was generally marked by the rise of the welfare state and welfarist protectionism. The aims of providing free and encompassing social, health and educational services were legally enshrined in various acts between 1945 and 1948. In respect to children these acts aimed to improve their well-being by providing universal health care, expanding education and producing better-off families. The Children's Act 1984 led to the establishment of local authority children's departments centralised by social services, marking the beginning of the child as a central aspect of social work and policy. Post-war legislation was based on new attitudes. Decisions were based on the new axiom of 'the best interest of the child', and society's treatment of its vulnerable members, such as children, was seen as indicative of the state of civilisation (Hedrick 1997; Stainton Rogers and Stainton Rogers 1992). However, legislation was also distinctly continuous in that children were still conceived through the discourse of innocence which constructs them as needing protection.

Despite a new discourse of children's rights emerging in the latter part of the twentieth century, the discourse of innocence prevails strongly to the present day, as reflected in legal measures and political actions. For example, the Protection of Children Act 1999 aims to identify and ban 'unsuitable persons', among them child sex offenders, from working with children (Cobley 2000). The Sexual Offences Act 2003 has created a new offence of 'grooming' children for sexual abuse, and automatically classified sexual intercourse with a girl under 13 as rape. Both acts conceive and reproduce children as innocent, vulnerable beings who cannot defend themselves and need adult protection. Indeed children under the age of 13 are deemed to lack (sexual) competence to such an extent that they are unable to give true consent to sexual acts.

The power of innocence

The continuing importance and strength of the discourse of innocence lies in its prevalence, its resistance to challenges and the ways in which it connects ideas of innocence and vulnerability. Both the media and focus group participants widely conceptualise children as innocent, immature, and lacking knowledge and skills associated with adults. The key lack is sexuality as children are defined by a lack of sexual knowledge, experience and desire:

Beth: My mum phoned the police [after Beth saw a flasher] and everything, and they were saying to me like, a ten-year-old, 'Did he have
a big erection?', and I was like. 'Uhh, what's that?', Do you know
what I mean, asking a *child*!

Judge Christopher Tyrer said: 'The victim of your sexual offences was
a child. She was **naïve** and **vulnerable** to predators like you. She was
a **virgin**, she had **no** previous boyfriends or **sexual** partners or experience. [. . .] Judge Tyrer said that he had passed a long sentence
because of the 'disgraceful betrayal of a girl's **innocence**'. (A.
Chrisafis, '5 years for a man who lured girl via internet', *Guardian*
25 October 2000, p. 7)

This innocence makes children naïve and vulnerable, and constructs
them as helpless victims in constant need of adult protection:

For too long the nation has endured the pain of seeing **innocents** such
as Sarah Payne snatched from streets to become victims of paedophiles. For too long not enough has been done to **protect** our **young
ones**. (Editorial, 'Our aim is the **safety** for our children', *NOTW* 23
July 2000, p. 6)

The pervasiveness of the discourse of innocence is occasionally inter-
rupted by the *Guardian* critically analysing it. For instance, the following extract identifies incongruence in government policies variably
built on concepts of children as active agents or passive victims:

[In] Labour's response to the paedophile scares and child abuse . . . the
emphasis is on children's **vulnerability** and dependence. Rhetoric
about predators is coloured by a sense that children are **victims**-in-
waiting. This leads to a puzzle: can the child who must not be allowed
out to play because of lurking dangers really be the same child exercising mature selection of subject and method in the classroom, the
same child thriving in out-of-hours classes so mum can work? (D.
Walker, 'Mixed-up kids: the government can't decide whether children
should be treated as **robust**, independent individuals or as **vulnerable**
victims-in-waiting', *Guardian* 28 August 2002, p. 17)

The author adopts a critical stance towards the discourse of innocence and ideas of vulnerability, mocking them through the neolo-
gism 'victims-in-waiting' which exaggerates their essence. This
extract illustrates a general difference between the *Guardian* and the
NOTW. The *Guardian* contains more articles questioning common
assumptions and a much wider range of views, with different opinions being expressed in editorials, feature articles, comments and

opinions columns. As a consequence the *Guardian* newspaper as a whole can appear contradictory and its readers are exposed to different perspectives. In contrast to this the *NOTW* is coherent and tends to contain *one* view throughout. Nevertheless, the above extract is an exception even in the *Guardian*. Overall the paper embraces and widely uses the discourse of innocence, emphasising its prevalence in two very different newspapers.

The power of the discourse of innocence also shows in its resistance to challenges, both experiential and research-based. In focus groups the idea of innocence is often contradicted, wittingly or unwittingly, through direct experiences with children. Yet ultimately the discourse of innocence is reaffirmed in the face of these serious challenges. For instance, participants share their experiences of their children possessing sexuality, in the sense that genital touching is interpreted as sexual curiosity and pleasure:

> Rachel: But are children not sexual?
> [silence]
> Helen: Yeah, they have sexual feelings, don't they, I've got a three-year-old and she touches her bum, so certainly she's got feelings down there.
> Hannah: My daughter's obsessed with her . . . vagina, and she's two and a half!
> Vic: My son's four and he's.. *always* got hold of his willy, *always* got hold of it.

Parents think of their children as sexual in some senses, and this thinking is shaped by mainstream discourses defining sexuality through genital stimulation and pleasure. Yet, while discourses on sexuality construct the children's behaviour as sexual, the discourse of innocence constructs children as asexual beings. This results in tensions and awkwardness, as indicated by silence. Discourses on sexuality make parents' direct experiences alternative because they provide an interpretation of children's behaviour which does not fit images of 'normality' produced by the discourse of innocence. Despite these challenges the discourse of innocence is upheld and reaffirmed, illustrating its power:

> Hannah: I believe in childhood.. and if you believe in childhood.. and if you believe in kind of childhood being **innocent** then.. and **innocent** being part of a **non-sexual**.. kind of life.

No matter what children do, no matter what alternative interpretations are provided, children continue to be understood as generally innocent and asexual beings. Thus parents see their children as sexual in *some* respects, but as asexual in many other respects, which can be made intelligible by looking at the *kind* of sexuality children are thought to possess. The social construction of sexuality and childhood means that children are neither inherently sexual nor asexual (Jackson 1982), generating significant space for varying definitions of sexuality. Parents' accounts confine children's sexuality to masturbation, i.e. sexual contact with the self. Therefore it is possible that they do not see children's sexuality as an expression of a wish for sexual contact with other persons. Moreover, parents do not seem to consider sexual activity in very young children sexual in the sense of intimate, seductive or shameful. Hence young children are allowed to carry out masturbation in front of parents but older ones are not:

> Rachel: But we draw a line then, don't we, sometimes, I'm, I'm sure I must have done it myself with my kids, I mean. . . my kids did that [touch their genitals] but then.. there must've come a time when I thought.. there's an age where.. either don't do it in front of me or don't do it in front of your friends or don't, don't.. you start putting all.. these barriers in.

Therefore children are granted sexuality but it is a kind of 'innocent sexuality' in that it is directed at the self only, automatic, unconscious and physical rather than affected. This may be why participants can simultaneously claim that children are innocent *and* sexual: their sexuality is not like adult sexuality.

The discourse of innocence is affirmed not only in the face of experiential challenges but also against research evidence. In the following article children are acknowledged to be knowledgeable and skilled at using the Internet, more so than many adults, and they are recognised to have internalised stranger-danger education. These acknowledgements should encourage a way of thinking about children as able to negotiate the Internet safely and provide their own protection. In this context the discourse of innocence, which constructs children as incompetent, should be questioned; but this is not the case:

> Children are becoming the internet experts in families as their parents leave them to it in what could be 'a lasting reversal of the generation gap', according to research published today. The report from the London School of Economics claims that warnings about the risks of

chatrooms and of meeting strangers and paedophiles have got through to youngsters, but that **parents, government departments** and **internet providers** could **do more to make the internet safer for children**. . . . They found that even in households with one or more computer-literate adults, children were often the internet **experts**. (R. Smithers, 'Children are internet experts', *Guardian* 16 October 2003, p. 5)

On the contrary, the discourse of innocence is reinforced through calls for adults to 'do more to make the internet safer for children', assuming and restating that children are in danger and in need of adult protection. This is incongruent with claims that children tend to be more skilled at using the Internet than their parents, illustrating the strength of the discourse of innocence as it cannot be disrupted by either research findings or direct experiences. This strength can be further illuminated through an analysis of connections between innocence and vulnerability.

Innocence and vulnerability
Christensen (2000) has argued that vulnerability is a *key* feature of Western conceptions of childhood. This vulnerability is socially constructed as well as biological. Although closely tied to innocence, vulnerability cannot be reduced to it because any childhood discourse can inform institutions (e.g. laws) and social practices (e.g. childrearing practices) which produce vulnerability. For example, the discourse of rights can produce vulnerability by exposing children to a neo-liberal society of competitive markets and individual responsibility (Lavalette 2005), while the discourse of evil makes children vulnerable by encouraging harsh forms of discipline and control (Jenks 1996). However, there is a particularly close fit between innocence and vulnerability which can be grasped through distinctions between different *kinds* of vulnerability.

Vulnerability as a generic term includes and conflates ideas of children as physically vulnerable (e.g. their bodies are smaller and weaker), socially vulnerable (e.g. they lack certain social skills) and structurally vulnerable (e.g. there are asymmetrical power relations between children and adults). Social and physical vulnerability tend to be seen as 'innate' characteristics of the individual child and denote a lack of individual, personal competence or strength. In contrast to this, structural vulnerability – as a lack of power – is a product of society. Discourses of rights and evil can produce structural vulnerability (i.e. they can render the child relatively powerless through social practices and structures) but they cannot produce children as innately vulnerable. This incapacity is grounded in (a) the structural perspective of the rights discourse, and (b) the innate characteristic of evil, which is fundamentally opposed to the characteristic of innocence. Hence the discourse of innocence is uniquely able to conceptualise and produce children as both structurally *and* innately vulnerable. By presenting children as lacking a range of social skills (e.g. being street-smart, able to judge dangerous situations etc.), the discourse of innocence constructs vulnerability as directly deriving from the being of the child. Innocence also produces children as structurally vulnerable, for instance by encouraging protectionist rather than rights legislation, but this kind of discursive effect is rarely acknowledged.

In the above extract the *Guardian* portrays children as technologically competent *and* innocent and vulnerable. Technological competence may not be easily transferred onto social competence, i.e. the kind of competence which could be argued to make children more clued up and less vulnerable. But the discourse of innocence is still problematic because it conflates innocence and vulnerability, and constructs both as innate characteristics. Any relative lack of competence and vulnerability should be understood in relation to the socio-structural position of the child where weakness goes hand in hand with adult demands for obedience (Kitzinger 1997). Children cannot be expected to shrug off obedience confidently in particular situations when it is generally encouraged as an aspect of the adult–child relationship. Children are expected to abide by their parents' rules, listen to their advice, and follow the instructions of other adults, such as relatives or teachers. Children do not have the same rights as adults, e.g. they have no rights to vote or to benefits (Qvortrup 2005). A legal ban on smacking children has been consistently opposed by many parents and the government in England, who foreground parental rights to discipline. Children's practices, decisions and ways of reasoning are generally not awarded the same status as those of adults because they are considered immature.

These structures make children relatively powerless and structurally vulnerable, and they promote compliance with adult wishes, rules and practices. Moreover, they can produce the kind of personal lack of social experience and social vulnerability which the discourse of innocence portrays as innate to children. As children are discouraged from being independent and gaining experiences their judgements of danger and acceptability may be impaired (Holloway and Valentine 2003).

The discourse of innocence is deeply implicated in the (re)production of these power structures by promoting a needs perspective foregrounding children's dependence. Children's needs are defined by adults and children's agency is constrained in the name of protection. By defining children through lack and absence (of adult competence), the discourse of innocence also renders children incapable of exercising many rights and undermines demands for equal rights. Paedophilia and child sexual abuse are offences which involve adults coercing children into sexual activity, and importantly the discourse of innocence does not protect children from abuse. Indeed it may be seen as producing vulnerability rather than protection. The discourse of innocence is implicated in the (re)production of unequal power structures which make children (structurally and socially) vulnerable, essentially producing structural and social vulnerability through conceptions of children's innate vulnerability. Further, the discourse of innocence is silent on the issues of lack of power and structural vulnerability, and this silence disguises its involvement in the production of vulnerability. As a consequence the discourse of innocence can continue to present itself as simply being about the protection of children, and this morally powerful position is further reinforced by circular discursive dynamics. The discourse of innocence conflates notions of innocence and vulnerability, as well as different dimensions of vulnerability, which means that the (structural and social) vulnerability it produces can be read back as a sign of innate innocence.

Sexuality and morality

As sexuality is tied to morality, the discourse of innocence is a fundamentally moral(istic) one. Innocence is the good norm prescribing that sexuality is a property children should not possess:

> Fiona: Children shouldn't have sex.

Linked to this are ideas on what 'proper' children are like. Certain forms of behaviour and ways of dressing are considered appropriate for children while others are not. The sexual dimension is the decisive factor as no sexuality is *the* structuring and defining absence. Inappropriate behaviours and clothes are those deemed adult-like, and clothes are defined as adult and inappropriate when they reveal parts of the body and/or possess sexual connotations, such as high heels or make-up:

> Kerry: I've been looking for like.. swimming costumes for Rachel [daughter] and they've got like these.. she's two.. tops there [illustration: handkerchief tops which cover the upper torso], all this stuff.
> Amy: Yeah the little triangle things.
> Kerry: And I'm thinking why?! She's two! Why does a two-year-old have to show her midriff? . . . And you see.. young girls.. whose fashion just replicates what the older.. teenagers and stuff are doing, and I'm sorry it's obscene. [. . .] And there's one, this girl [in a TV singing contest].. had hair up like this, lip gloss, make up out here.. and she was only ten.. and some kind of outfit on, heels that thick, and you just thought 'Why?'.. and she had a fantastic voice, she did, but it spoilt it because of all this.

Practices and products which reveal parts of the (naked) body or possess sexual connotations count as 'sexy', and laments disregard the fact that many of these items are mass market products which position children as major consumers.

Concerns about the effects of 'sexy' practices and products are clearly gendered as they focus on girls only. This is rooted in risk perceptions in focus groups being generally gendered, with girls often being considered more 'at risk' than boys. These perceptions rely on traditional concepts of femininity as weak and vulnerable, and masculinity as strong and powerful (Oakley 1972). However, there is also a sense in which sexiness, especially in conjunction with beauty and seductiveness, is itself a gendered concept. Despite masculinity arguably being increasingly connected to beauty and health regimes (Mort 1996), femininity has a long history of being deeply intertwined with ideals around the body beautiful. Participants may be encouraged to complain about girls' sexy appearances because the very idea of being sexy and seductive through beautification is still more easily applied to females than males. This tendency is to an extent rooted in the fact that sexual innocence is itself a gendered concept; in our contemporary culture it is mostly girls who are eroticised, and girls are always already (hetero)sexualised as part of 'normal' femininity and girlhood. Hence, boys' expressions of (hetero)sexuality are rarely pathologised and only girls invoke social anxieties when they consume products or engage in behaviours associated with 'older' female sexualities, such as wearing high heels

(Renold 2005). Combined with the virgin/vamp discourse of femininity, gendered notions of sexiness and sexual innocence produce the concept of females endangering themselves through seduction (Benedict 1992), which further fuels anxieties about girls', rather than boys', displays of sexuality and sexiness.

These issues raise questions about the relationship between 'sexy' and 'sexual'. Focus group participants conflate the two concepts so that 'being sexy' and 'being sexual' become synonymous. The discourse of innocence constructs children as asexual in the sense of lacking sexual knowledge or experiences, but it seems that even sexy clothes indicate a sexual child. Through these conflations examples of 'sexiness' become sufficient to invoke complaints about the contravention of 'appropriate' childhood behaviour and dress. Notions of (in)appropriateness, of right and wrong, are fundamentally moral and normative and offer opportunities of moralising. In this case affect is conveyed through exclamations and questions (e.g. 'And I'm thinking why?!'), and serves to represent oneself as a moral person who would never let such indecency happen because of strong notions of right and wrong.

The most defining characteristic of children is an absence – no sexuality – hence the negative approach of defining children by what they do *not* or should *not* possess. Conversely, the presence of sexuality spells the end of childhood. In a very literal way paedophilia and child sexual abuse are often conceptualised as the end of innocence and childhood, as the defining essence of both, asexuality, is being 'destroyed':

> **Our society** must be . . . protecting our children from the most vile criminals in our midst, the paedophiles. At present . . . children are exposed to attacks that result in murder or else **rob them of their innocence** and leave them traumatised into adulthood. (F. Broughton, 'Every policeman backs campaign', *NOTW* 20 August 2000, p. 6)

However, child sexual abuse is not even needed for people to declare the end of childhood. Because of conflations of 'sexy' and 'sexual', sexy clothes or demeanours are sufficient to announce the loss of innocence and childhood:

> Amy: I mean S Club Juniors, that's awful the way they are.. they're acting like they're adults.
> Jack: Yes, and that's wrong because their.. their childhood innocence will be lost.. in that sort of development.

Like the 'destruction of childhood' concept, rape (of adult females) tends to be understood through a narrative of the social death of the victim (Phoenix and Oerton 2005). According to the authors rape does not need to occur as even *threats* of sexual violence are considered sufficient to induce this experience. The child sexual abuse discourse seems to go one step further by removing the need for any *connection* to attack, violation, threat or abuse as a basis on which to pronounce the death of childhood and children. Children's displays of 'sexiness' or 'sexuality' are sufficient.

Any destruction referred to in the focus group examples above is of course not real but metaphorical; at stake is not the physical harm done to children because an element of physical harm is not even necessary to talk about the end of childhood. The outrage and condemnation people express towards paedophiles can therefore only partly be about real violence against real children. It is also, and perhaps more importantly, about the symbolic violation of the much-valued concept of childhood, the violation of adult norms and morals. This confirms Douglas's argument that we can explain the risks selected for attention and fear in any given social form through values. The more widely and deeply these values are held, the more likely they are to be selected as a great risk. 'Common values lead to common fears' (Douglas and Wildavsky 1982: 8), and childhood innocence is a *very* common value. Left open is the question why the asexuality of childhood is such a strong value.

Generally speaking, participants see adulthood and childhood as essential, separate and mutually exclusive categories. Any blurring of strict boundaries, the crossing of the dividing line of asexuality, spells the end of childhood. Transgressive incidents include not only sexual clothing, demeanour or abuse but also sexual appreciation of children by adults:

> Kerry: The minute they [adults] start looking at young children in that sort of.. a way.
> Amy: It's not children anymore.

Essentialist conceptions and strict dividing lines produce a simplistic understanding and easy moralising where anyone sexually appreciating children is a paedophile and any child with some kind of contact with sexuality or sexiness is no longer a child.

There are many problems with these simplistic conceptions and their consequences. For instance, Kitzinger (1997) has pointed out that childhood innocence is itself a sexual commodity, a source of titillation for abusers, and this is exploited by companies to market and sell their products (e.g. adult school uniforms). Therefore, the promotion of the notion of innocence is far from unproblematic, and the dividing line between sexuality and innocence becomes more than blurred as the two aspects are directly linked in some ways. The extension of the neo-liberal market has exploited this link and profited from the commodification of childhood innocence, but this is largely ignored or denounced as immoral. No one, including neo-liberals, backs the commodification of childhood innocence, even if this is contradictory. One cannot generally champion the market and its profit logic as the best regulator of social life, and condemn it when its logic extends to virtually all areas of life. Commodification involves the provision of a product on the market in such a way that it is saleable to consumers, e.g. it must appeal and have a price which consumers are willing to pay (Leys 2001). From this we can infer that there is a market for products appealing and titillating through childhood innocence, which suggests that it is not uncommon for adults to see children as sexual objects, sexual beings and sources of sexual pleasure. But this is exactly what is denied through the discourse of innocence and the figure of 'the pae-dophile', and produces a contradiction in governance, between the laissez faire neo-liberal extension of the market and the state regulation of childhood.

The discourse of innocence is not only problematic because it conceals the complex connections between innocence, sexuality and sexual abuse. Concepts such as childhood asexuality and the loss of innocence also raise the question of whether any child who does not conform to the image of the 'proper child', in terms of looks, behaviour or lack of sexuality, is still a child. If children and childhood are *defined* by innocence then the answer is no. The concept of innocence is a double-edged sword, which stigmatises the sexually aware, knowing child and makes offences against it less serious (Kitzinger 1997). This tendency is comparable to portrayals of rape where women considered 'sexual' (in terms of their clothes, demeanours, history of partners etc.) are turned into amoral vamps who have provoked their victimisation (Benedict 1992). Ashenden (2004) suggests that the ethical problem of child sexual abuse is predicated on the sexual innocence and vulnerability of children; this tendency to ground moral condemnations of sexual offences in the nature of the victim is clearly problematic, for concepts of these 'natures', e.g. innocent children or virginal women, always imply the existence of 'other' children and women who are not as pure and therefore turned into 'lesser' victims. However, children are never held responsible for sexual violence committed against them in the same way that adult women are, due to a paradigmatic 'blameless victim' status generated by the discourse of innocence (Davis 2005). Rape myths such as women provoking or deserving rape (Benedict 1992) are also not easily applied to children because the discourse of innocence constructs them as asexual, immature and naïve. Hence, displays of sexiness or sexuality tend to be read as imitations of adult behaviour rather than enticements to sex, and children cannot be blamed for being in 'risky' situations as they are supposedly unaware of the existence of risks.

The stigmatisation of 'knowing', i.e. sexually aware or experienced, children suggests that the category of childhood does not contain all children, because it is defined by adult ideals of what children *should* be like. However, the argument that the category of childhood is preserved through the removal of 'errant' children is most persuasive in the case of violent children (Jenks 1996). Sexual abuse of children is interpreted as the end of childhood but sexually abused children continue to be represented as innocent, for instance in the media or legal cases. These tensions are the result of opposing tendencies to exclude and include. The general tendency in the media and the public – as focus groups above indicate – is to exclude children who do not fit in order to preserve images of innocence. But the sexually abused child is the paradigmatic, blameless victim who deserves inclusion (Davis 2005). As a consequence, sexual abuse can be pronounced the end of childhood and yet sexually abused children continue to be seen as innocent and remain part of the childhood category.

These inclusion–exclusion dynamics are structured along the lines of childhood, morality and gender. Those children whose transgression has been forced upon them and who are therefore not to blame, e.g. the sexually abused child, tend to be included. Those whose transgression of the ideal can be interpreted as wilful and their fault, for example children who display 'sexy' clothes or demeanour, can be excluded. However, exclusion is mediated by gender in the sense that only girls' displays of sexuality or sexiness tend to be pathologised (Renold 2005). Moreover, even such 'deviant' children are often still included in the category of childhood as the blame for their transgression is shifted onto the adult agencies considered responsible, such as parents or governments:

> I cannot believe some of the things I see **little girls** wearing. Any child's party these days is likely to yield a crop of lisping Lolitas in **boob-tubes, mini-skirts** and **high heels.** Even more upsetting are **black lace knickers, G-strings** and **padded bras** with the Little Miss Naughty logo. It's a paedophile's dream come true. And by dressing our kids so provocatively we're handing it to them on a plate. [. . .] So any **man-ufacturer** who encourages that situation is unbelievably irresponsible. . . . **Parents** who try to resist these sick trends find themselves under incredible pressure. . . . Of course we have to assume some responsibility but so do **retailers.** (U. Jonsson 'Our kids shouldn't be dressed to thrill', *NOTW* 25 September 2005, p. 21)

It is also important that the non-sexual characteristics captured and ascribed by the discourse of innocence – such as vulnerability or weakness – are actually reinforced by the event of child sexual abuse because the characteristics of victimhood and childhood greatly overlap. Hence child sexual abuse to an extent affirms children *as* children, which again encourages the tendency to include children who have been victims of sexual violence but not those who 'experiment' with sexuality or sexiness.

As childhood and sexuality are socially constructed, children are neither inherently sexual nor asexual (Jackson 1982). My critique of the concepts of innocence and asexuality has been informed by their troublesome implications, and it has focused on asexuality because of its contemporary cultural dominance. Any critique should not be interpreted as supporting sexual relations between adults and children; the unequal power structures in current society are not conducive to reciprocal and autonomous sexual relations between them (Giddens 1992). At the same time we have to emphasise that the powerful equation of asexuality with protection is misconceived.

Being a child, being at risk

When children are conceived of as innocent and vulnerable then they are by implication at risk. As this 'at-risk' status is grounded in the nature of the child – constructed as naïve and lacking adult skills by the discourse of innocence – being a child becomes synonymous with being at risk. As a consequence, risks are omnipresent and children, who cannot provide their own safety, need constant adult protection:

> Hannah: The minute you have a child . . . you can't take safety for granted.. anything can happen to your child.

> Claire: And you think.. when you're not with them, then you never know what might happen.

The idea of children needing protection pervades the whole debate on paedophilia and is often indirectly present as it is simply assumed. For instance, parents educate their children about stranger danger and restrict their Internet access, participants want access to the sex offender register, and disapprove of parents who do not always supervise their children to ensure their safety. The underlying assumption is always that children need protection, that they are too vulnerable, immature and naïve to provide it themselves. The latency of these logical links within the discourse of innocence illustrates their power. They possess such a truth status that they can simply be assumed, do not have to be explained, and are rarely challenged. No one will publicly question if children really need protection.

Paedophilia is constructed in terms of paedophiles being a risk to children, and the discourse of innocence constructs children as being *generally* at risk. As a consequence, not all children are seen as equally innocent or at risk from paedophiles. Innocence and risk are positively correlated so that the more innocent a child is, the more at risk it is. The major factors structuring assessments of innocence and risk are age and gender. Age is crucial as it represents a marker and boundary of childhood. Teenagers are seen as different from children and/because they are acknowledged to have sexual experiences, which participants consider acceptable from between 13 and 16 years of age onwards. Central to acceptance of teenage sexuality is the notion of consent: unlike children, teenagers are considered mature enough to give their consent:

> Tanya: Well, a lot of 13, 14-year-olds are already.. sexually active **of their own free will**.

To that extent age negatively correlates with innocence and risk: the older a child, the less innocent and at risk it is seen to be. However, significant age gaps between sexual partners rouse suspicion that no real consent was given by the younger partner because of power differentials, putting her or him at risk of abuse. Teenage sexuality has to take place between teenagers to be deemed acceptable and non-abusive:

> Claire: Even though a 15-year-old girl, yes, shouldn't be having sex, 15-year-old girls have sex with 15-year-old boys.. is that a crime? . . . If they both do it.. together.. then it's not.. so bad.

Therefore age structures risk through both the age of the child (teenager) and the age of the sexual partner, and age structures intersect with gender structures. For some people the risk of paedophilia is gendered as boys are seen as less at risk than girls. Others consider both sexes equally at risk because risk status is rooted in the position of the child rather than gender. These different attitudes emerge clearly in the discussion on whether an adult female having sexual contact with a 15-year-old male can be classified as child sexual abuse:

> Kerry: And that female teacher that, from Canada, that was having sex with them 15-year-old lads.
> James: But if you're a 15-year-old lad you'd be well chuffed.
> [everyone laughs]
> Kerry: When I read that I thought the woman was abusing the child, I'm sorry that's just child abuse.

For James the relationship is acceptable because the child is male and indeed the thought of classifying it as abusive is ridiculed, while for Kerry it constitutes child sexual abuse. For Kerry the power differentials between child and adult are crucial and define the relationship as abusive, while for James the child–adult power relations have been counterbalanced by traditional gendered power relations. These are built on physical power differences and traditional views of masculinity (defined by activity, conquest and sexual pleasure) and femininity (defined by passivity and peacefulness). The implications are that females cannot physically force males into a sexual relationship, and that males always want and enjoy sex (Oakley 1972). Thus while the overwhelming discursive presence of innocence means that children are generally conceptualised as being at risk, this risk status is mediated and structured by the age and gender of the child (teenager) as well as the sexual partner.

The discourse of rights

The latter half of the twentieth century arguably saw the rise of a new discourse of childhood focusing on children's rights. In contrast to the needs discourse associated with innocence and protectionism, this discourse sees children as active beings with interests in their own right. The rights discourse is about children *doing* things while the discourse of innocence is about children having things *done to* and *for them* by adults. The rights which are demanded for the child are general rights to adult respect and participation, which would enable children to express and assert their interests *themselves*. The child is seen as structurally rather than inherently weak, due to the adult world putting children at a structural disadvantage. The language of the rights discourse centres on the empowerment and autonomy of the child (Lansdown 1994; Roche 1996).

In political and legal terms there have been a number of fragmented moves towards increasing children's rights. On an international level the UN Convention of the Rights of the Child in 1992 listed and prescribed a number of children's rights in the areas of provision, protection and participation. On a national level the Children's Act 1989 is most commonly associated with the legal championing of children's rights. Its groundbreaking potential lies for example in giving children the possibility of engaging in legal proceedings without guardians, and in imposing a duty on solicitors to take instructions from the child rather than the guardian under certain circumstances. This act does provide new ways for children to express their own interests, but these are restricted by adult decisions on children's maturity to make use of them, and by the power of the law to restrict children's autonomy by deciding against their wishes (Lansdown 1994; Roche 1996). Children's rights have also been strengthened by the 1985 requirement for doctors to provide contraceptive advice to children without parental knowledge and the abolition of corporal punishment in state schools in 1986 (Bell 1993b). Further examples of the rise of the rights discourse concern the new Children's Rights Movement which contains a growing number of agencies campaigning for children's rights rather than protection, such as the Children's Legal Centre or the Children's Rights Development Unit or EPOCH (End Physical Punishment of Children) (Hendrick 1997). Overall, the law can be seen as increasingly concerned with children's interests and feelings, yet such moves are fragmented and contradictory, as legislation which is protectionist and/or undermines the autonomy of children continues. For instance, the Criminal Justice Act 1991 has restricted the entitlement of teenagers to social security (Bell 1993b) and the Sexual

Offences Act 2003 states that children under 13 are unable to give consent. Thus the legal and social impact of the discourse of rights is fragmented and varied.

The media and the crisis of rights

In the focus groups the discourse of children's rights did not feature at all. The case for the discourse of rights in the media is complex, complexity indicating a crisis of neo-liberal governance over who should possess which rights. The *Guardian* very rarely understands children through a discourse of rights. The sample of this media study is of course limited but the absence is still surprising given the paper's politics and liberal concern with civil rights and liberties. Moreover, the rights of any other social group involved in pae-dophilia controversies are considered, such as released sex offend-ers, parents, employers, employees or citizens generally.

The following excerpt, written by an academic guest columnist, is a rare occurrence. It considers children as independent beings and the implications of independence, such as conflicts of interest between children and parents:

> Yet children have fewer **rights** in our society than we do, and policies which affect them profoundly are rarely framed in terms of their **needs**. [. . .] There are many good childminders, but in childminding legislation, too, the **rights** of children come last. This government has stuck defiantly to its policy of letting minders smack if parents agree, so that one child can be legally hit but not another. There is no right to equal treatment: it is parents' 'right' to decide. Similarly, it is their 'right' to decide on a child's education and beliefs: in the debate about faith schools, while parents' rights were posed against issues of social inclusion, nobody mentioned the **rights** of children themselves to edu-cational equality. (J. Williamson, 'The neglect we tolerate: children have no political power, so their needs and experiences are ignored', *Guardian* 22 June 2002, p. 22)

Nevertheless, even Williamson slips back into the discourse of inno-cence. The lack of children's rights is seen to matter by producing a situation in which children's needs are not catered for by adults (e.g. 'policies which affect them profoundly are rarely framed in terms of their needs'). Thus children are ultimately seen as beings with special needs; they remain passive and their rights are not to *do* something but to not have certain things *done to them*. This moving between discourses illustrates the power and pervasiveness of the discourse of innocence in our culture; it is difficult to get away from thinking about children in terms of needs. This way of thinking tends to subsume children automatically under agencies which provide for these needs – either parents or the state. The ascribed conditions of need and dependence discourage conceptions of children as a group of persons with independent selves and capable of agency.

In the *NOTW* the discourse of rights is more prominent than in the *Guardian* because paedophilia is framed within a polarised discourse of rights. This discourse juxtaposes paedophiles' rights and children's rights, as well as parental rights and authorities' rights. Children's rights to free movement, not being threatened and a carefree childhood are seen as systematically infringed by paedophiles' rights to free movement, definite sentences, parole and privacy. As a consequence the rights of both groups are represented as mutually and directly exclusive:

> We are taking the first step to publish the names and addresses of known sex offenders. . . . There will be the usual squawks of protest about **civil liberties** and **civil rights** from those who make a living **taking the side** of the **criminals**. Well, what about the **liberty** of an eight-year-old child to walk through a field of wheat in high summer? What about the **rights** of a boy or girl to spend childhood NOT looking in fear over their shoulder? (Editorial, 'Our aim is safety for our children', *NOWTV* 23 July 2000, p. 6)

While the *NOTW* in this instance frames the debate as a conflict of rights, my argument is that children are not *really* thought of as beings with rights, despite the occasional use of such terminology. Rather the *NOTW* instrumentalises the language of children's rights for its own ends. It uses it to oppose children to paedophiles and declare their rights incompatible, i.e. to present the world as simply about good and evil, and ruled by common sense. This polarised discourse of rights serves a number of purposes. It justifies the disentitlement of paedophiles from human rights and facilitates a critique of authorities and liberals as unnecessarily intellectual, lenient and concerned with the rights of offenders, i.e. as on the 'wrong side' (e.g. 'those who make a living taking the side of the criminals'). Further, it allows the *NOTW* to present itself as good and moral, as fighting on behalf of parents and children (e.g. 'Our aim is safety for our children').

The *NOTW* tends to conflate the discourses of rights and needs, which suggests that the two are interchangeable for the newspaper, synonymous in their meanings. Children are not genuinely understood as independent beings with rights but simply talked about as having rights/needs which remain defined and secured by adults through protection:

> This idea of naming the perverts is very simple. It says in essence that the **protection** of children is more important than the **privacy** of paedophiles. [. . .] Children must be **free** to run free and play safely without fear. (S. Arnold et al., 'Parent power can change law', *NOTW* 30 July 2000, pp. 2–3)

As a consequence children remain needy and incapable, which is opposed to a true discourse of rights which conceptualises children as active, strong and competent. A genuine discourse of rights is further undermined by the *NOTW* tying the rights of children to the rights of parents:

> The priority should be the **protection** of children and not the **privacy** of paedophiles. [. . .] It is every parent's **right** to have controlled access to information about . . . convicted child sex offenders who may pose a risk to their child. ('Sarah's Law', *NOTW* 13 August 2000, p. 6)

These connections assume that the interests of parents and children are identical, again contravening a true discourse of rights which conceptualises children as independent. Of course the *NOTW*'s campaign is also not about rights for children but about the protection of children through rights for their parents, the right to community notification. The 'name and shame' campaign is marketed as a campaign for parent power, not child power. Thus the *NOTW* cannot really be seen as understanding children through a discourse of rights, despite its use of rights terminology.

The rights case in the *NOTW* is complex: rights are conflated with needs, the rights of different groups are seen as identical, and certain people are seen as having no right to rights. This complexity signifies a crisis of neo-liberalism. The concept of rights is central to the philosophy of neo-liberalism, which sees the individual as having the right to freedom in the sense of self-determination, as opposed to regulation by the state. Individuals should be free to choose, act in their own interest and pursue their own goals (Kabeer and Humphrey 1991). As markets are seen as providing these opportunities, market rule and neo-liberalism have even been seen as ultra-democratic and liberating. They offer unlimited choice for everyone. This market populism is of course flawed; consumer choice is tied to financial resources so that certain sections of society are excluded from choice. Further, ideals of democracy, freedom and human rights cannot be reduced to consumer choices where the only choice and right is to buy or not to buy (Frank 2001). Paedophilia, with its disputes about the rights of different social groups (parents, child sex offenders, the government, children etc.), indicates a crisis of this neo-liberal philosophy. Its focus on individual rights and their championing through market rule do not work, as different social groups possess different, often incompatible, interests. These have to be balanced, as everyone exercising their right to choose any course of action would result in anarchy. But the market recognises instrumental rationality as the only working principle and thereby reduces humanity to a series of instrumental transactions, devoid of collective sentiments, interests and values (Carrier 1997). Consequently, the issue of balancing divergent rights and interests in the name of the greater good needs decisions based on ethics and values, and cannot be solved by the market. The government has no coherent ideas as the market has become its philosophy and the end result is confusion over rights: who can and should be allowed to exercise which rights, when, where and under what circumstances.

This confusion over rights is most pronounced in the case of the state versus the family. In one sense this dilemma is not novel and is grounded in the complicated relationship between liberalism and the welfare state (Ashenden 2004). The state wants to promote free agency and the autonomous family and to respect individual rights and privacy. But at the same time it cannot opt out of its responsibility to ensure and protect the wellbeing of its citizens, which necessarily involves state intervention into their private lives, and curbing certain individual freedoms in the name of the collective interest (Dingwall et al. 1983). In the welfarist post-war years the state comes to take care systematically of the upbringing of children and the protection of their physical and mental wellbeing (Hendrick 1997; Stainton Rogers and Stainton Rogers 1992). This welfare model necessarily implicates the state interfering with the sphere of the family which is traditionally considered to be autonomous. This intervention is often indirect as the state defines the responsibilities of parents and concepts such as 'adequate upbringing', but the state also directly intervenes into families considered unfit or inadequate in the care of their children. Interventions are usually meant to help the family; however, the state does have great powers such as the removal of children (Dingwall et al. 1983; Parton 1991).

Since the inception of the welfare state the balance between children's and parents' rights, child protection and adult liberties, has been a major concern and point of dispute in the public, the media and the social services. This dispute about the responsibilities of the state versus the autonomy of the family presents a dilemma for all governments. They are unable to satisfy a public which simultaneously asserts that not enough is done to protect children and complains about the interference of meddling social workers (Dingwall et al. 1983; Parton 1991). However, if contemporary confusions over rights and responsibilities are to some extent a feature of post-war history, they are also much more pronounced and marked by hostility than previous debates. This is not surprising. Welfarism has always included support for individual rights as well as state interventions in the name of collective interests. In contrast to this, neo-liberalism practically reduces state intervention and provision to the bare minimum, and ideologically denounces state regulation as inefficient and wrong in the sense of infringing individual rights and freedoms. Against this backdrop the current government then wants to sell its policy on paedophiles, which entails the restriction of the right to access information on sex offenders to the state, as necessary and good. This issue causes much confusion and antagonism because it blatantly reveals to the wider public the irreconcilable contradictions in the government's philosophy and actions.

Making sense of concern with paedophilia

Sacralisation and sexuality

This brief history of discourses of childhood has outlined a historical shift from a discourse of evil to a plurality of discourses. In debates on child sexual abuse and paedophilia children are overwhelmingly understood through a discourse of innocence, and occasionally the discourses of evil and rights are invoked to explain certain aspects of paedophilia (e.g. false allegations or the provision of legal rights). An earlier attitude of indifference appears to have given way to care and protectionism; the economic child has become the emotional child. Further, children have moved from obscurity to the centre of the family, and become the focus of social policy and law. These shifts have been noted by several authors and described as sentimentalisation (Steedman 1990), sacralisation (Zelizer 1985) and the imputation of specialness (Jackson and Scott 1999).

Zelizer (1985) offers the most sustained of these interpretations. Looking at public responses to accidental deaths in the US in the early twentieth century she notes two things. First, responses to child deaths are more intense and indignant than responses to adult deaths as the killing of a child is seen as a moral offence, a sacrilege. Second, child mourning has been magnified and organised, for instance in child safety campaigns and child memorials. Child deaths are not just personal tragedies but matters of public concern. For Zelizer this sensitivity is grounded in and can be explained through a cultural transformation of the meaning of children. This transformation is termed the sacralisation of the child, a process by which the meanings and values of the child have shifted from economic worth to emotional pricelessness. Since the start of the twentieth century, she argues, children have become sacred beings invested with religious and sentimental meanings. The point here is not that people previously lacked sentiments towards children but that now the child is valued exclusively in emotional terms. Indeed, economic and emotional/sentimental values are seen as incompatible. Like Ariès (1962), Zelizer links these developments to the rise of the family as a sentimental institution and the domestication of (middle-class) women through full-time motherhood. The consequences of this sacralisation are considered detrimental as children become too dependent, over-protected, oversupervised and domesticated – the place of the sacred child is either indoors or in designated, protected public places.

Zelizer's ideas on the sacralisation of the child are valuable in that they offer to explain the outrage accompanying paedophilia, and the fact that any risk or danger to children is conceived as particularly serious and unacceptable (Jackson and Scott 1999). Moreover, the concept of sacralisation illuminates the attitudes of focus group participants. For instance, several participants believe that crimes against children are more important, severe and serious than other crimes (against adults):

> Abi: That crime's a lot more important as well, isn't it.. than any other crime that's.. gonna be reported about, I mean.. crime, paedophilia.. with children.

This common perception suggests that children do have a special, valued status: violating children is considered particularly morally base and causes concern and outrage. Thus the concept of sacralisation can explain the condemnation and hostility directed at paedophiles through paedophilia being a crime committed against children, the special and sacred beings. Yet this concept cannot explain why paedophiles in particular should become the focus of social concern now, and why this concern should be so persistent and intense. The physical abuse of children for instance attracts by no means the same levels of concern and outrage today. Thus the concept of sacralisation offers to explain a social predisposition to be concerned about (risks to) children but it cannot explain why attention focuses on some dangers at the expense of others, or indeed the timing of such attention.

The rationalisations of focus group participants suggest that condemnation of paedophilia and child sexual abuse is grounded in the combination of the innocence of children and the sexual nature of the crime. In their explanations of why crimes involving children are particularly bad, participants point to children being innocent, defenceless and vulnerable:

> Anneke Meyer (A. M.): How would you compare crimes against children with crimes against adults?
> Sinead: I think it's different because **adults can defend themselves**, they *know*, kids don't, so I think it's worse.
> Donna: Yeah, cause kids are **innocent**.

Participants here conceptualise crime as an interpersonal power struggle between two individuals. Understood on the basis of individual conceptions of power, this struggle is unequal when it involves individuals with different 'amounts' of power. Commonsense perceptions of power often identify it as physical strength; however, participants here also conceptualise power as deriving from knowledge (about sexuality). The weakness of children makes crimes against them 'worse' than crimes against adults because the struggles involved appear unequal, unfair and cowardly. Targeting those who cannot even fight back seems particularly morally reprehensible:

> Fiona: And I think any sort of sexual crime is quite bad but.. I think with children it is particularly bad because they do seem so **innocent** and so.. **vulnerable**.

Such legitimations suggest that the sacred status of the child gains its moral authority from the discourse of innocence, which constructs children as virtuous and vulnerable beings, and thereby renders them 'pure victims' (Davis 2005). But the discourse of innocence constructs children as weak, vulnerable and defenceless in more than one way; children are portrayed as lacking a range of skills, experiences and strengths such as physical strength, social skills and sexual knowledge. Among the many crimes against children child sexual abuse can be understood as particularly reprehensible because it arguably exploits several dimensions of children's vulnerability, most notably their lack of knowledge about sexuality as well as their physical weakness.

Aside from innocence and sacralisation, sexual violence fuels condemnation of paedophilia:

> Miles: OK, is a paedophile worse than rape then? Paedophilia?
> Kerry: Cause it's sex with children Miles.. it's sex with *children*, it's.. it is.. that violence, it's not just sex, it's.. it's violence against children . . . *sexual* violence against children.

Sexual crimes (whether committed against adults or children) are generally seen as particularly serious in our culture due to a number of factors. They involve physical violence against a person, and a violation of what is seen as the most intimate sphere of the body. According to Foucault (1978) sexuality is seen as the defining essence and truth of the self, and in that sense sexual crimes seem to violate a person in a particularly profound way. When children are involved, the severity of sexual violence is aggravated by the discourse of innocence. It defines asexuality as the essence of childhood, which turns child sexual abuse into a crime violating the essence of the victim, and renders it a 'worse' crime than child physical abuse or sexual abuse of adults. In addition to the physical harm inflicted in all cases, sexual abuse of children is 'unnatural' in the sense of forcing experiences on to children which 'nature' had not yet intended:

> Fiona: When you hear about a sexual crime between.. a grown man and a grown woman.. it's still really bad but.. because adults have sex anyway . . . but when you hear about sexual crimes to children it's *sick*.. it's so different.. because **children shouldn't have sex**.

Again, indignation focuses on the metaphysical, moral rather than physical violation, the 'destruction' of childhood rather than children. Moral violation is what marks paedophilia out as special, as 'sickening', as 'worse' than other crimes.

Recent proposals by the ex-home secretary David Blunkett to change crime sentences are also a good indicator of the importance of both sacralisation and sexuality in explaining social reactions to paedophilia. In 2003 he proposed the creation of indeterminate 'life means life' sentences for those who kill an adult or a child in the following circumstances: *multiple* murders involving a high degree of premeditation, abduction or sadism. These sentences would also apply to the *single* murder of a child involving a high degree of premeditation, abduction, sadism or sexual conduct. The importance of sexuality is emphasised by sexual murders being rated as worse than non-sexual murders. Further, the proposals reveal that children have a more sacred status than adults as crimes against them are rated as deserving tougher sentences than those committed against adults. A single murder of an adult in the same circumstances as mentioned above will 'only' gain a 30-year prison sentence (Travis, 8 May 2003). The specifications of sexuality and abduction also strongly suggest that this law is really aimed at paedophiles. Linking this back to neo-liberal forms of governance, proposals again illustrate that paedophilia and sexual offences against children are governed in very interventionist, authoritarian and punitive ways, which are incongruent with the neo-liberal philosophy.

On the basis of participants' rationalisations and government laws we can hypothesise that paedophilia is considered such a horrendous crime because it is a crime which is sexual and committed against children. Both aspects, sacralisation and sexuality/sexual violation, are further aggravated by the discourse of the innocent child. Paedophile crime violates two deeply held and cherished views: that children are sacred and that children are sexually innocent, and it might be this mix which makes paedophilia so potent in raising emotions. The dynamics between innocence, sexuality and violent crime turn paedophilia into a veritable atrocity. Yet this does not explain why the focus should be on stranger paedophiles rather than child sexual abuse in the family. The hypothesis also implies that there is an element of hypocrisy in social reactions to paedophilia as the emotions expressed are only partly about the harm inflicted on children, while real indignation is rooted in the destruction of concepts which adults value. This could explain why outrage and debates focus on offender types, paedophiles, rather than offences committed. No matter what the particular offence entails, paedophiles always violate the concepts of the sacred child and sexual innocence; if this is what the indignation is about then the details of the offence become unimportant – violation has occurred, and that is what matters.

The moral rhetoric of childhood

Generally speaking, the concept of sacralisation proves to be powerful and pervasive, showing itself indirectly in many ways. For instance, demands for tough punishments reveal how children become central to a moral rhetoric which can legitimise anything without actually having to explain it. Capital punishment and indeterminate sentences are only seen as appropriate for those committing crimes against children:

Jack: Once they've been classified as paedophiles, that's it.. ehm.. locked up.. and they stay there . . . once someone's interfered with a child that's serious enough.

Donna: That [reintroducing capital punishment] would be a *start*, wouldn't it, that would be a start.. cause that's [paedophilia] the most heinous crime of all, that's what they [paedophiles] deserve.

Sinead: If someone kills a child, I want it [capital punishment] for that.

This raises the question of why crimes against children should deserve harsher punishment. Children in themselves are not a proper explanation but they can come to function *as* an explanation because they immediately invoke ideas of children being special beings. 'The child' becomes a shorthand for sacralisation whose meanings no longer have to be made explicit. In fact, *any* opinion can be justified by simply referring to children without having to explain why and how children justify it. This includes justifying assessments of crimes against children as particularly serious:

James: You've got to be really careful though, cause it's **obviously** like one of the most emotive issues [paedophilia], that's like people don't like seeing murders and stuff on TV, we do, but **obviously**.. when seeing kids go missing, obviously they think it's worse.

In this case James cautions against quickly labelling people as paedophiles because of the emotive reactions which this label invokes. The media reference in this context is an interesting reminder of just how mediated and televised people's experiences of crime are, especially of crimes like paedophilia which are prominent in the media.

Children are also used in focus group debates to legitimise a general prioritisation of policy matters in favour of children:

> Jack: They spend all these resources on.. stupidities like speed cameras . . . when it comes to children . . . I think it should be a priority, that they spend more money on that, on the kids' side of things.. so we are protecting them rather than.. you know, trying to get a guy who's not driving his car.. with any car tax.

They justify public access to the sex offender register:

> Beth: I think the residents should know if there's one [paedophile] in the area.
> Fiona: Yeah, cause they're kids.

And legitimise even violence towards paedophiles:

> Tanya: There's a few that would be aggressive to that paedophile.
> Sinead: But if you do something like that to a child what do you expect?

All these different extracts show how children can be directly used as an explanation for a wide range of opinions: 'it's because of children'. Children absolve the speaker of the necessity to provide specific explanations for *how* the involvement of children supports their argument. The high frequency of occurrence of words such as 'obviously' demonstrates that children are widely accepted and understood as an explanation. Perceptions of the special status of the child are so deeply and widely entrenched as to appear 'natural'. At this point of being 'natural' a discourse becomes most powerful; gaining the status of an irreversible, 'natural' fact it can conceal its social construction. It is because of this 'natural-fact' status that children can become an explanation, and the power of the concept of sacralisation shows most strongly in the moral rhetoric of childhood.

If the moral rhetoric of childhood is fundamentally grounded in invoking the sacred status of the child, sacralisation itself gains moral authority from the discourse of innocence. By portraying children as entirely virtuous, the discourse predisposes them to become the objects of emotional and moral valuation. Children are the *deserving* recipients of attention, care and protection. This is why children can be declared a priority, and participants can use such declarations to present themselves as moral persons. Anyone who speaks on behalf of children can represent himself or herself as a moral person, i.e. somebody who protects the weak and vulnerable. Childhood rhetoric is always moral rhetoric, and as a consequence *anything* can be justified via children. Children make the case necessarily good and right.

However, while demands for the safety of children in the media and focus groups are quite generalised, the issues of child protection and prioritisation are raised in specific contexts. There is a hierarchy of crimes in terms of interest and seriousness, as only certain social issues, phenomena and behaviours are selected and constructed as *major* social problems (Cohen 1972; Douglas and Wildavsky 1982). The *NOTW* for example is extremely preoccupied with paedophilia, yet there are many dangers facing children which are not as high on its agenda. Jack's comment above revealed this hierarchy clearly in comparisons between traffic offences and paedophiles: some crimes are deemed more severe and worthy of prosecution than others. These selections and hierarchies indicate the explanatory limits of the theory of sacralisation. First, not all crimes against children are considered equally severe, so that the moral rhetoric invoking the sacred status of the child varies in terms of its power. Second, it can explain the societal predisposition to be concerned about issues affecting children but not why sacralisation 'works' to translate this predisposition into *major* emotive concerns in some cases but not others. As noted above, we can speculate that the reasons lie in paedophilia being a crime which is sexual, interpersonal and intentional, and that the sexual nature of the crime is aggravated by a discourse of the innocent, asexual child.

Modernity and late modernity

Contemporary concern with child sexual abuse and paedophilia has been linked to modernity. For Jenks (1996) the conceptual shifts towards the child as an ideal being are intertwined with the modern project of the Enlightenment. The child in modernity, he argues, is understood through modern discourses of growth and progress in the sense that children's potentials have to be facilitated to achieve the promise of a better future. The idealised discourse of innocent, virtuous children represents the manipulation of certain images of children to achieve ends beyond children, to finish the modern project. In relation to modernity Jenks suggests three factors which have encouraged the preoccupation with child sexual abuse. First, with modernity attitudes to children have become more caring and watchful, which might have lowered the threshold of tolerance to abuse. Second, child sexual abuse has been politicised, most notably through the child protection movement. Third, while modernity has freed the child from adult identity it has not freed it from the adult world. Child sexual abuse is a continuous phenomenon which has not been eradicated by modern progress, and which is problematic for modern society because the treatment of children is seen as symbolic of the social order, as indicative of the moral state of society.

The child protection movement certainly plays an important role in ensuring that child sexual abuse remains a high-priority issue. For example, in January 2004 the children's charity NCH (National Children's Homes) published a research report concluding that the Internet had led to a phenomenal 1,500 per cent increase in the consumption of child pornography and caused a rise in child sexual abuse cases (e.g. *Daily Express*, 13 January 2004; Wilson, 13 January 2004). The NSPCC has for years run the 'Full Stop' advertising campaign which features graphic reconstructions of neglected and abused children. Such actions aim to combat child sexual abuse but also maintain it as a public topic and social problem: they draw attention to it, suggest that it is a large-scale problem, induce guilt and indicate moral responsibility.

The principles of the Enlightenment are reason, rationality and progress. This research has shown that addressing child sexual abuse is indeed seen as an indicator of the enlightenment and the progressiveness of society:

> Hannah: I think we talk about it [child sexual abuse] a lot in this country . . . in Cyprus it probably happens just as much but people.. don't talk about it, you know.. maybe it's a blessing that we hear about it because people can talk about it.

At this point we can go beyond Jenks to suggest that once this belief is in place, child sexual abuse might be perpetuated as a social problem because people can use talking about it as a way of representing themselves as enlightened and progressive. Jenks points to a contradiction in such views, though: if society is so progressive why has child abuse not been eradicated? This dilemma should curb any moralising, but instead it is resolved in ways which safeguard moralising.

First, the above example shows that the dilemma is resolved through comparisons of the UK with other countries, which serve to portray this country as relatively progressive and morally superior. Second, this contradiction can be made intelligible through social class bias. The problem of child abuse is located in the lower social classes who are understood as not having made the kind of progress typically associated with the Enlightenment. The lower classes are seen as physically abusing their children because low levels of intelligence and education lead to an inability to reason with children and recourse to violence:

> Celia: But also there's a class thing, as well.. you know, we do.. I mean this idea of a classless society is farcical, we do have differences in class, different classes, and you know.. you have to say, you know, people who *reason* with their child, you know.. and then you have people who won't reason, who just, you know.. have different levels of physical abuse.

This suggests that child abuse can be seen as pre-modern *and* prevalent in contemporary society if it is 'accounted for' through social class divisions. This reconciliation might work better for physical than sexual abuse of children, though, because the former, by being obviously physical, is more easily associated with violence and the lower classes. Both ways of resolving the dilemma of continuing child abuse in modern society are ultimately forms of locating the problem 'outside' or with the 'Other', either other countries or other social groups within society. This strategy reflects the exclusionary dynamics Jenks (1996) identifies in the preservation of the category of childhood. The removal or displacement of unfitting, 'other' or deviant elements in order to preserve widely cherished categories and images seems to be a feature of child (sexual) abuse controversies in more than one way.

Modernity, according to Jenks, encourages a preoccupation with child sexual abuse but the condition of late modernity offers the real explanation for concern. Late modernity is characterised by a pragmatic state of disenchantment where dreams, utopias and confidence have been lost. Individual experience of late modern life is one of discontinuity and contingency. The self has become reflexive, and fixed parameters of social living have been eroded and the usual points of attachment shaken up. However, Jenks argues, people still want continuity, coherence and secure attachments. Drawing on

Beck (1992) he suggests that in this context concern with children has to be understood as a form of nostalgia and a private type of re-enchantment. The disorienting change makes adults cling to children as the last unconditional, stable relation, and as a symbol of past times of care, trust, dependency and love that we long for. Child sexual abuse attracts such attention and outrage because to abuse a child means to strike at the last remaining vestige of the social bond, the last symbolic and nostalgic refuge for such desires.

Some focus group participants certainly displayed a strong sense of nostalgia; they longed for childhood as a time of dependency, carefreeness, closeness to nature and joy:

> Beth: I remember now having, rolling down the hills, being stupid.. acting like a baby, laughing me head off.. and I thought 'I just wanna run down hill, I just want to be free.'
> Donna: Be a kid again.

These nostalgic notions emerged most strongly in a group where many participants had children at a very young age. They displayed an acute sense of parenthood curbing their freedom:

> Sinead: When you're older you regret not doing things when you're young, when you do have time to do.. and you should be like.. having fun and that, it's too late once you start having kids and everything.. it's not the same.

For these participants childhood and adulthood are two dominant life phases, which follow each other without any significant interval phase, i.e. the beginning of parenthood marks the end of childhood. Because of a lack of an interval phase – in which participants are neither child nor parent – freedom is firmly located in (their own) childhood, and loss of freedom is associated with the beginning of parenthood. Nostalgic images of childhood are therefore not simply an expression of a longing for trust, dependency and care (gained from children), but also an expression of a longing for freedom and a lack of responsibilities (here children are a burden). This somewhat complicates Jenks's explanation. If concern with child sexual abuse is rooted in a nostalgic clinging to childhood then this clinging occurs because of *and* in spite of children, because of glorified memories of childhood and an equation of childhood with being child-free.

There are several questions which neither Jenks's nor Beck's ideas can explain, such as why child sexual abuse and paedophilia rather than other risks attract such attention. Their models only provide explanations for a general predisposition to be concerned with threats to children. Explanations also rest on the fundamental but questionable assumption that flux, ambivalence and instability necessarily create anxiety, even though these states can also be interpreted as liberating. The late modern mood of disenchantment arguably represents a disillusion with modernist ideals and ways of structuring life, but this mood does not really square with popular demands for a strong, interventionist, protective, punitive, i.e. modernist state, demands which are displayed in paedophilia debates. Thus the explanatory value of these theories is too broad and general to account fully for concern with paedophilia. Theories rely on interpretations, which are possible rather than necessary, contentious and so large-scale that they are difficult to evaluate empirically.

Conclusions

The discourse of innocence dominates the understanding of paedophilia in the law and government, the media and the wider population. Its dominance is reflected in its pervasiveness and resistance to challenges, whether experiential or research based, and is partly grounded in the close connections of ideas of innocence and vulnerability. Outrage about child sexual abuse is rooted in concern with both the physical violation of children and the symbolic violation of the moral and normative concept of childhood innocence, a concept generated and cherished by the adult world. In this sense concern is not simply altruistic or an indicator of morality but rather an opportunity to represent yourself as a moral person. This opportunity is grounded in the moral dimension of the discourse of innocence. The sacred status of the child arguably allows for childhood to become a moral rhetoric, and turns issues affecting children into moral issues. The opportunities for representing yourself as moral by appearing to speak on behalf of children help explain the *perpetuation* of paedophilia as a high-profile topic. Other explanations for emotive reactions to paedophilia include the equation of being a child with being at risk, and a social predisposition to be concerned about children which is rooted in the sacred meaning of the child. Yet there are plenty of risks affecting children, and in order to explain why society focuses its interest and emotions on *particular* issues it is necessary to look at the specific aspects involved in these high-profile issues. In the case of paedophilia the combination of children and sexuality is a very potent one as the involvement of either in a crime 'exacerbates' the generally serious incident of crime. The involvement of both does not simply double this impact but multiplies it, as the discourse of innocence turns sexual crimes against children into unnatural atrocities. Hence, the social hierarchy of concern and interest has to be explained through issue-specific factors, but their meanings and power seem to remain deeply connected to childhood and morality. The next chapter will take these issues further by exploring the construction of the figure of 'the paedophile' and locating fear in the dangerousness of this discursive figure.

3

Figures and fears: discourses around paedophilia and the dynamics of concern

According to Kincaid (1998), gothic narratives are central to social reactions to paedophilia and child molesting. Paedophilia, he argues, is a story based on the binary opposites of monsters and angels, evil and virtue, perversity and purity, sunshine and darkness. Hence, paedophilia takes the form of a gothic narrative in which paedophiles represent evil and children goodness. Similarly, Cohen (1972) has suggested that moral panics contain a folk devil, i.e. an entirely negative, evil, demonic figure, which terrifies and which is central to the process of media manufacturing of fear. There is nothing positive, human or even ambiguous about folk devils, and 'the paedophile' has been claimed as a classic folk devil of our time (Critcher 2003). Both perspectives, gothic narratives and moral panics, suggest that social understanding and reactions are characterised by processes of categorisation and demonisation. The problem, paedophilia, is seen as embodied by a particular social group, paedophiles, which is othered and vilified, represented as simply evil and having nothing to do with 'us'. Consequently, individual paedophiles can be known and recognised as instances of the type or category. The concerns generated by the issue of paedophilia are located in the monstrous nature of the key deviant, 'the paedophile'.

In contrast to this, Bell (2002) has suggested that in contemporary controversies around paedophilia, paedophiles are *not* understood as types and categories but simply as individuals. This lack of categorisation is inferred from observations that there are no longer any attempts by the media, by academics or in the wider culture to explain child sexual abuse(rs) theoretically. Paedophiles are arguably simply seen as unknowable individuals. Moreover, the

NOTW's 'name and shame' campaign in 2000, which included demands for public access to the sex offender register, can be interpreted as a demand for *specific* information which enables children and parents to avoid specific individuals. General knowledge and theories, Bell argues, are dismissed as useless because criminals remain unknowable. It is presumably this inability to know and recognise paedophiles which makes them so dangerous and able to incite fear: if we cannot identify a danger it is impossible to protect ourselves from it. This forms the basis of the populist appeal of the *NOTW*'s demands.

Different theoretical approaches prompt the question of whether paedophiles are knowable or unknowable, categories or individuals, types or anyone, devils or humans. I want to argue that they are both. The ways in which the media and focus group participants construct 'the paedophile' are both categorising and universalising, typifying and individualising, demonising and retaining a human dimension. Further, I want to locate the dangerousness of the figure of 'the paedophile' and its ability to incite fear precisely in these contradictions, in the incorporation of binary opposites. Simple negativity or unknowability can arguably not capture the complexity and dangerousness of the figure of 'the paedophile'.

These arguments are explored in this chapter through a detailed discussion of the different concepts and discourses which are involved in the construction of 'the paedophile'. There are four major discourses – evil, perversion/pathology, violence/destruction and cunning – which are used to understand and describe paedophiles. In these processes certain personal, psychological and behavioural characteristics are attributed to paedophiles, who become a type of person with typical mindsets and behaviour patterns. Discourses serve to construct 'the paedophile' semantically as a discursive figure and to categorise; typification represents paedophiles as a specific and 'other' category of people, a kind of person different from the rest of society. However, 'the paedophile' also remains a distinctly human figure and unknowable individual, for example in terms of appearance or cognitive skills.

Evil

Paedophiles are constructed through a discourse of evil (e.g. Collier 2001; Kitzinger 2004). The *NOTW*'s coverage of paedophilia is permeated by references to paedophiles as possessing a thoroughly wicked, malicious and evil nature, devoid of any positive or ambiguous attributes. From a gothic narrative perspective, the evil of 'the paedophile' is generally constructed in relation to the goodness of the child. The oppositional nature of the connection means that the two figures reinforce each other, e.g. the goodness of the child emphasises the bad, amoral nature of 'the paedophile' (see Chapter 2). Specifically, paedophiles are produced as evil through the application of lexical items (nouns, adjectives, adverbs and verbs) which directly associate them with the realm of the satanic, including 'devil', 'evil', '(sex) fiend', 'depravity' and 'vicious'. These constructions are forms of categorisation and demonisation. Paedophiles are not only portrayed as marginal, evil 'Others' or persons but excluded from the category of humanity by being associated with and placed in the realm of the satanic. The *NOTW* expresses and produces the concept widely by using adjectives to qualify the subject, paedophiles, as evil:

> For these **evil** perverts there must be no hiding place. (Editorial, 'Help hunt for Sarah', *NOTW* 16 July 2000, p. 6)

Further, the *NOTW* uses terms such as 'evil' as nouns. In this process of nominalisation the noun replaces the subject so that evil does not just become a *characteristic* of the subject but literally *the* subject itself:

> **Evil** on the loose. (A. Gekoski, headline, *NOTW* 9 November 2003, p. 32)

In contrast to the *NOTW* the *Guardian* only rarely brands paedophiles as simply evil:

> Last night's Concorde crash and the killing of Sarah Payne expose the powerlessness of the human condition. We are helpless. [. . .] They are far apart, these two moments of calamity. One feels random and unavoidable, a natural disaster; the other an **act** of deliberate **evil**. [. . .] The murder of Sarah Payne . . . was no accident. It was the product of a human decision to do harm – an **act** of the **devil**. (J. Freedland, 'When death strikes', *Guardian* 26 July 2000, p. 15)

And when it does there is a tendency to make the terminology of evil more acceptable by intellectualising it, for instance by putting it into a 'philosophical' context of the 'powerlessness of the human condition'. While the term 'devil' suggests personification, the *Guardian* tends to describe the *acts* of certain paedophiles rather than individuals themselves as evil. Acts define and produce a person, but by not being synonymous with *the* person they leave some scope for change or alternative characteristics. The focus on evil acts is not as sensational, totalising or demonising as the *NOTW*'s constant personifications and nominalisations of evil.

Further, in contrast to the *NOTW* the *Guardian* occasionally features articles directly speaking out against portraying paedophiles as evil demons:

> I have spent much time with child abusers, murderers and, most recently, men accused of rape. What strikes me whenever I encounter those regarded as beyond the pale of humankind is how very **ordinary** they are. They are simply men (and mostly men) who have committed criminal acts, often so horrific they seem unforgivable. **That does not, however, make them devils or monsters. They are neither essentially different nor utterly evil.** You would be surprised how kindly and well behaved they are in every other aspect of their lives apart from the crime they have committed. [. . .] There is a **potential for good and bad in nearly everyone,** not only a few. (D. Birkett, 'Names that hurt', *Guardian* 6 July 2000, p. 20)

The production of paedophiles as evil is therefore actively challenged as a process of demonisation, the concept of the evil person is rejected and the ambiguity of human nature is emphasised. The different uses of the same concept within the same paper reflect a general tendency of the *Guardian* to contain a much greater range of voices than the *NOTW*. So while the *Guardian* does to some extent produce paedophiles as evil this production is significantly less pervasive, straightforward and strong than in the *NOTW* due to less usage, less sensational usage (no nominalisations, evaluation of acts rather than actors, fewer headlines), and a greater range of opposing voices.

Understanding in focus groups parallels understanding in the media in many ways. Some participants conceive and reproduce paedophiles as evil through the application of terms conveying such meanings, e.g. 'evil', 'depraved', 'depravity', 'bastards' and 'mean':

> Kerry: I don't know how you can cure that sort of **depravity**.

> Donna: Dirty, **evil** bastards.

However, this understanding is not as common as it is in tabloids, and like the liberal *Guardian* openly liberal participants focus on and are careful to label acts rather than people, offences rather than offenders:

> Hannah: I'm not convinced they're [paedophiles] all these evil bas-
> tards, you know, kind of thing.. what they *do* is evil but I'm not con-
> vinced that that *is*.. holistically evil.. completely evil.

This phenomenon can be interpreted in different ways. Evil is a dis-course people easily associate with paedophiles, yet the focus on offences means that evil is seen as an aspect of the subject rather being the subject. Moreover, the concept of evil is reproduced rarely, and in contemporary culture it is very difficult not to be aware of it, whether one agrees with it or not. Awareness should not automati-cally be equated with acceptance, and indeed Hannah's above comment represents a critique of contemporary culture's tendency to see paedophiles as entirely negative people. Individuals can obvi-ously reject and disagree with certain media opinions. However, this example also illustrates the power of the media, and the wider culture, to provide the discursive framework for expressing argu-ments and negotiating opinions. Whatever your personal opinion, you have to think and talk about paedophiles in terms of evil; this is exactly the power of discourses (Mills 1997).

Animal terminology

The discourse of evil demonises paedophiles in the most literal of senses as they are constructed as outside the category of humanity through positioning in the realm of the satanic. More specifically paedophiles are produced as inhuman through the association with terms usually reserved for animals, such as 'monster', 'predator/predatory paedophile', '(sex) beasts', 'lurk' or 'prey'. In the *NOTW*, articles and headlines are littered with animal terminology:

> Scouting out the **beasts**. (Headline, *NOTW* 23 July 2000, p. 5)

> The British public have spoken and they back us to the hilt – we must
> have Sarah's Law to protect our children from **predatory paedophiles**.
> [. . .] These are real people with real fears about **monsters lurking** in
> their communities. [. . .] The information needed by worried parents
> will cover only those paedophiles who repeatedly **prey** on children and
> pose real danger. (Editorial, 'The nation is backing vital campaign –
> the evidence is overwhelming.. we must have Sarah's Law and end
> killing', *NOTW* 25 August 2002, p. 6)

This terminology produces knowledge about paedophiles by suggesting how paedophiles behave and how to interpret that behaviour. For instance, a male trying to talk to two females accompanied by small children is understood as 'preying' on children and consequently as a danger:

> Beth: We were there [Piccadilly Gardens, Manchester] one day and we all got chips, sat round, and kids running into and out of the fountains.. and this fella kept looking.
> Donna: Yeah, why **prey** on.. innocent young kids?

The situation in the *Guardian* is again more complex because some terms are acceptable whereas others are not and contexts of deployment vary. There have also been terminological changes over time, for instance terms such as 'beast' or 'prey' have been shunned in the *Guardian* until recently, while the terms 'predator' and 'predatory' have been fairly common since 2000. These terms do construct paedophiles as animals, but they are used in ways and contexts which make them more acceptable and less sensational. The *Guardian* emphasises that the terms refer to a certain category of people by dividing paedophiles into different categories:

> From the brief time-span, he [police detective] knew that if Sarah had been taken, it was by a specific type of paedophile: a **'predator'**, who snatches swiftly, rather than a **'groomer'**, who acts after cultivating a relationship with a child. (S. Hall, 'Brother may have seen kidnap van', *Guardian* 8 July 2000, p. 4)

Categorisation renders the use of terms like 'predator' respectable; it makes them appear official and scientific, part of the scientific endeavour to differentiate, classify and explain. This effect is also achieved by attributing the terms to claims-makers with status, such as a police detective. Wider contexts render animal terminology less inflammatory, for instance the term 'predator(y)' is not used in the *NOTW* context of beasts and monsters.

However, regardless of context such terms are categorising and objectifying as they construct paedophiles as a distinct and subhuman breed. The metaphorical exclusion of paedophiles from the category of humanity makes obsolete any potentially troubling issues, such as how similar paedophiles are to 'normal' people, allowing for the world to be understood through a simple 'us versus them' paradigm. The focus groups illustrate this as some participants take dehumanisation to its logical conclusion by identifying paedophiles literally as animals and objects rather than human beings:

> Sinead: They [paedophiles] should have a [tracking] device, the way dogs have in their ears, were you can tell where they always are.
> Donna: You can put them on cars why can't you put them on paedophiles?!

Animal terminology produces knowledge of paedophiles as inhuman and this understanding translates into and legitimises demands for inhuman treatments and the denial of basic human rights:

> Kerry: The day he became a paedophile, was the day he gave up his right to some sort of privacy.

> Claire: I don't think.. their human rights should be considered cause I don't think they're human.

Thus the discourse of evil, constructed and reproduced by different media and individuals to different degrees, categorises paedophiles as inhuman and produces an understanding of them as both animal-like and satanic. This can shape practices (e.g. participants avoid contact with those whose behaviour is interpreted as 'preying'), worldviews (us versus them), and certain demands and solutions (see Chapter 5).

Perversion and pathology

Paedophiles are commonly defined and categorised through their sexuality, their sexual preference for children:

> He [a convicted paedophile] does not expect people to understand why he was **sexually attracted to boys** as young as eleven. (N. Hopkins, 'Child abuser speaks out over mob fury', *Guardian* 11 August 2000, p. 11)

The focus is on paedophiles as persons rather than their actions or offences, and sexuality becomes the key to group identity. Paedophile sexuality is known through the closely linked discourses of pathology and perversion, which are derived from psycho-medical science (Howitt 1995). While both discourses normatively produce paedophile sexuality as deviant and abnormal, there are differences. The discourse of perversion is openly moral and constructs paedophiles as sick and perverted. This is reflected in popular nouns used to describe paedophiles, such as 'pervert' or 'perv', and common adjectives (expressive values) such as 'sick', 'vile' or 'disgusting'. In comparison, the discourse of pathology is more acceptable because it lacks such sensational terminology and is associated with a pseudo-medical approach classifying paedophilia as a disease which people have to be cured of. In contrast to medical implications of a cure, however, the popular understanding asserts that one can neither understand nor change nor cure paedophiles: once a paedophile, always a paedophile. Thus paedophiles are an eternal risk.

The discourse of perversion and the figure of 'the pervert' are generalised in the sense that they are circulated around various sexual criminals and forms of 'deviance', such as rapists or men with sexual fetishes. 'Pervert' or 'perv' are the key words encapsulating this general discourse and figure, and they are widely used in the *NOTW* and the focus groups to understand and produce paedophiles as perverted:

> **Pervert's** back in old haunts. (A. Gekoski, *NOTW* Headline, 27 August 2000, p. 17)

> What to do if there is a **pervert** on your doorstep. (T. Taras and P. McMullan, *NOTW* 23 July 2000, p. 2)

However, the discourse of perversion is also constructed through much more detailed statements, themes and beliefs, which are specific to understandings of paedophilia. Paedophilia as a form of sexuality is said to be an obsessive, compulsive lust, which makes those afflicted incurable and drives them to reoffend indefinitely:

> And, secondly, it [community notification] is based on the premise that **never in history has a paedophile been cured. They will re-offend.** (S. Arnold et al., *NOTW* 'Parent power can change law', 30 July 2000, pp. 2–3)

> Sarah: They [paedophiles] don't stop at one [child], whenever the opportunity arises.. they're gonna have that feeling again.

These forms of knowledge produce paedophilia as a permanent condition and paedophiles as a permanent risk:

> Donna: They [paedophiles] never change.

> Claire: They [paedophiles] can't stop themselves.

> Tanya: Yeah, many of them [paedophiles] just *are* like that.

These constructions also produce 'the paedophile' as fundamentally different from 'ordinary criminals', and as a consequence ordinary penal measures such as determinate sentences or rehabilitation we presented as failing as effective solutions:

> But when it comes to child molesters, the fundamental assumptions of the justice system are still wrong. [. . .] **Abusing children is not like nicking cars or breaking into people's houses.** (S. Simon, 'Dos get a dose of right medicine', NOTW 30 July 2000, p. 11)

> Donna: I mean paedophiles you can't treat them, it's in them.

The only effective measures are those which permanently remove 'the paedophile' from society, such as capital punishment or lifelong incarceration:

> Jack: No.. no, no.. once that's [paedophilia] in your mindset that's it, you just got to lock them up.. forever.

The discourse of perversion, in all its facets, is commonly used and produced in the *NOTW* as well as focus groups, suggesting that it is deeply entrenched in our culture. It is a very moralistic and normative discourse which entails expressions of disgust. Adjectives and nouns such as 'sick', 'deviant', 'dirty' or 'disgusting' suggest repugnance, and foster the production of paedophilia as abnormal and deviant:

> Sarah: They wanna do it to children.
> Sinead: That is just **sick**.

The figure of 'the paedophile' is constructed in relation to the figure of the innocent child. It is the sexual innocence of the child which makes sexual attraction to children so abnormal, unnatural and wrong as to call it sick and deviant. The figure of the child, marked by asexuality, turns the figure of 'the paedophile', marked by sexual attraction to children, into an abnormal 'pervert':

> Karen: It's just **not normal** to want to have sex with a *young* child.
> Jack: No it's not, definitely not.

Despite the extensive overlap between media discourses and focus group discourses, however, there are limits. The second focus group did not understand paedophiles through the discourse of perversion at all, possibly because all the vocal participants in this group read liberal broadsheets only. Such readers are likely to be aware of the concept and terminology of perversion but unlikely to want to associate themselves with its crudity, anti-intellectualism and anti-liberalism. Individuals' politics may shape the impact of media discourses. Widespread views of paedophile sexuality as extremely powerful, compulsive and permanent almost construct paedophiles as slaves to their sexuality. Despite this the media and focus group participants consider them fully capable, responsible and culpable.

The *Guardian* did not seriously deploy the discourse of perversion in 2000, and instead understood paedophiles through a discourse of pathology. Many focus group participants also subscribed to this discourse, showing that unlike the media, where newspapers tend to use *one* discourse, individuals mix discourses. The discourse of pathology constructs paedophilia as a disease, illness or condition which afflicts people:

> James: I think it's [paedophilia] a **mental illness**.. it might.. it should be classed as a mental illness.. basically.

> Claire: I do think they're [paedophiles] sick, they *are.. sick*, they're not well.

This discourse is never challenged as the *Guardian* and focus group participants widely understand paedophilia as an illness which needs to be cured and talked about in medical terms. However, some of its implications are disputed, for instance there are debates over whether it is possible to cure paedophiles:

> Hannah: I don't believe you can actually *cure*.. certain.. things.
> Helen: Sexual abusers . . . need.. some sort of **therapy**.

Other participants question and reject the discourse's provision of a medical explanation for paedophilia as an excuse:

> Sinead: It's like if you say 'Oh, I'm sick.. it's not my fault', then it's ok.. you're allowed away with it.

In all debates the underlying and undisputed belief is that paedophilia is a disease, and the power of the discourse of pathology clearly lies in this capacity to set the framework for debate. You can discuss the possibilities of cure, extents of recidivism and whether pathology as an explanation implies exoneration, but you have to talk about and accept pathology as the founding parameter and 'truth'. Recidivism becomes an issue because the discourse of pathology, while being less condemnatory and sensational than the

discourse of perversion, is still a normative one producing paedophilia as a deviant sexuality, and paedophiles as likely recidivists
driven by this abnormality:

> The chief probation officer points out: '[. . .] In these circumstances it
> is harder for the police to exercise surveillance, or to involve them
> [paedophiles] in treatment programmes which can control their
> **deviant sexual tendencies.**' [. . .] Lord Bingham ruled: 'While the **risk
> of repeat offending** may in some circumstances justify a very limited
> measure of official disclosure, a general policy of disclosure can never
> be justified.' (A. Travis, 'Paedophile row: vigilance – or vigilante
> justice?', *Guardian* 24 July 2000, p. 3)

In contrast to the *NOTW*, the *Guardian* frequently considers the
possibility of paedophilia, as a form of sexuality, being controlled
through treatment. But the focus is on control rather than cure, possibility rather than certainty, and recidivism remains understood as
very likely. Thus paedophiles are still produced as a permanent risk,
if not as big or 'certain' a risk as in the *NOTW*.

Like the discourse of evil, the discourses of pathology and perversion categorise paedophiles by attributing certain sexual desires
and behaviours as typical to them. They are othering and normative
but not as simply demonising as the discourse of evil, as they present
paedophiles as ill rather than satanic.

Changes in terminology: the *Guardian*

The *Guardian*'s coverage, compared to the *NOTW*, can generally
be described as more comprehensive, diverse (encompassing different viewpoints) and less inflammatory. Its terminology is often different, some tabloid terms such as *predator* are used but in different
contexts. However, between 2000 and 2003 terminological changes
took place, which will be analysed using the terms 'beast', 'monster',
'prey' and 'pervert'. I will argue that this typical tabloid terminology, which was largely shunned or mocked by the *Guardian* in
2000, had become acceptable by 2003. For example, in 2000 the
Guardian used the words 'monster', 'beast' and 'pervert' solely ironically to ridicule tabloids:

> There's a **pervert** on my doorstep. . . . It's only two days since The
> News of the World published his name and photograph in its list of
> child-sex **monsters**. . . . Some people must surely hope that he hasn't

read the paper, watched the news or met anyone in Londis who put two and two together. Otherwise, this unique opportunity to bag the **beast** closest to them will have been lost. [. . .] The only potential problem with this plan was the danger that some dense soul might misuse the **beast** list for purposes other than 'knowledge' and that these same individuals might well prefer to pour petrol through the letterboxes of their chosen **perverts** than just stick their faces up on the fridge. . . . According to the News of the World's editorial, the only proper response to discovering a **beast** in your midst is to forget you found him. (C. Raven, 'Pervert special – buy the set: the News of the World's real motive behind the publication of its paedophile list', *Guardian* 25 July 2000, p. 5)

Irony is achieved in several ways: by overusing tabloid terminology, extending and exaggerating it through alliterations (e.g. 'bag the beast'), or neologisms (e.g. 'beast list'), and by stressing the illogical nature of the *NOTW*'s actions and justifications.

Despite this open disdain for tabloid terminology, by 2003 the *Guardian*'s attitude had changed. Words such as 'beast', 'monster', 'pervert' and 'prey' were no longer considered inappropriate and

1 *Guardian*, 10 October 2003

were used seriously, if rarely. For example, a major story on the conviction of Douglas Lindsell in October 2003 carried the head-line 'The perfect family man who **preyed** on young chatroom girls'.

The article stated:

> Yesterday [. . .] Lindsell was exposed as the world's most prolific inter-net groomer. Detectives revealed that, posing as a teenager, the pen-sioner had **preyed** on more than 70 girls across the world in internet chatrooms. [. . .] Even after he was caught and police confiscated his computer, he logged back on to the internet via digital television and carried on grooming girls. [. . .] The case once again exposes the danger of paedophiles using internet chatrooms to groom vulnerable young girls. (S. Morris, 'The perfect family man who **preyed** on young chatroom girls', *Guardian* 10 October 2003, p. 3)

The term 'prey' is used without any qualification, hint of doubt or irony. The general context differs from that in tabloids, e.g. sen-tences are often longer and there are words which would not be used in tabloids such as 'confiscate'. Yet there is also a sense in which this coverage has got quite a tabloid feel (Jucker 1992; Simon-Vandenbergen 1986). By the *Guardian*'s standards many sentences are short and have a simple syntax (subject–verb–object construc-tions), which presents all matters as facts and the world as a straightforward place (e.g. 'The case once again exposes the danger of paedophiles using internet chatrooms to groom vulnerable young girls') (Fairclough 1989). There is no questioning, no indication that statements are *claims*, and no references to the sources of claims. Moreover, this tabloid feel is caused by the size and nature of the image. The article frames a nearly A4-size mugshot of Douglas Lindsell which conforms to many stereotypes of paedophiles in terms of looks, e.g. scruffy, unkempt or old. Underneath the photo-graph the caption describes Douglas Lindsell as an 'internet menace', an expression which emphasises danger through objectifi-cation and portrayal of an individual as a significant threat.

The *Guardian*'s use of tabloid terminology is not confined to news articles. In the following editorials the context of coverage is typical of broadsheets. Terms like 'grooming' are put in quotation marks, the pros and cons of technological developments are considered, and the editorial calls for a debate rather than drastic measures. In the middle of this the term 'pervert' appears:

Microsoft's decision to close its unmoderated UK internet chatrooms
will be greeted with relief by parents all over the country. [. . .] These
sentiments will be echoed by millions of people in the wake of a series
of scandals in which paedophiles and other **predators** have used internet chatrooms to make contact with children in order to 'groom' them
for subsequent meetings. [. . .] Technology has opened up much
greater opportunities for **perverts** (however small in number relative
to internet users as a whole) but also offers sophisticated technologies
to track paedophiles and other sexual offenders down as a recent spate
of arrests indicates. [. . .] It is not an easy call. A serious debate is
urgently needed. (Editorial, 'No room for doubt', *Guardian* 24
September 2003, p. 23)

The context influences the impact of the term 'pervert', making it less
sensational. What the *Guardian* means by 'pervert' also does not
seem to be exactly the same as what the *NOTW* understands by it, if
we take 'pervert' to be a generic term indicating 'paedophile'. This is
due to differences between the two papers in terms of discourses and
frequency of use. For instance, the *Guardian* mostly understands
paedophiles as pathological persons committing evil acts, and the
acts are sometimes classed as perverted. The *NOTW* understands
paedophiles consistently as inherently and purely perverted evil.
Nevertheless, it is remarkable that terminology has changed over time
as terms such as 'pervert' have become acceptable in the *Guardian*.

There are no obvious reasons for these developments, but they are
another indicator of a lack of a liberal discourse on paedophilia as a
true alternative to the populist discourse. The *Guardian* is not as sensational and paedophiles are not as simplistically demonised, e.g. the
discourse of pathology is usually preferred over the discourse of perversion, or the discourse of evil is applied to acts rather than people.
But these are nuances. Overall the *Guardian* understands paedophilia through the same discourses as the *NOTW*, and if this produces more nuanced knowledge and understanding it does not add
up to alternative understanding and knowledge. For example,
understanding paedophiles as pathological rather than perverted still
produces them as abnormal, in need of change and difficult to cure.

Violence and destruction

Violence is another important discourse in the construction of paedophilia. Paedophiles are portrayed as violent and destructive, as

willing to abuse, violate and kill children simply for the satisfaction of their lust. A terminology denoting and connoting violence is used to describe paedophiles and their actions, e.g. 'snatch', 'attack', 'abduct', 'assault', 'damage', 'violent' or 'aggressive'. The discourse of violence is used and produced in both newspapers but much more common in the *NOTW* than in the *Guardian*:

> Too many children are being **damaged**. (Editorial, 'You spoke, now they are all listening', *NOTW* 6 August 2000, p. 6)

> They [paedophiles] cause the **deaths** of too many children and **wreck** the **lives** of far more, all for the satisfaction of selfish lusts. (D. McKie, 'Elsewhere: child-killers on the loose', *Guardian* 7 September 2000, p. 19)

It culminates in the belief that paedophiles violate children to such a degree that they are left traumatised. The consequences of paedophile crimes are portrayed as endless and too terrible ever to be really overcome:

> He sneaked into the house one night, woke the youngster up and dragged her to his caravan where he carried out a series of **vile attacks** on her, **bound** and **gagged** her and tried to **rape** her. [. . .] Now 16, the girl has never got over the **trauma** of that night. She has twice tried to commit **suicide**. (J. Staples, 'Vicar's wife begs News of the World to save family from fiend', *NOTW* 13 August 2000, p. 4)

The meaning and impact of the discourse of violence are grounded in its connection with sexuality, as sexual crimes tend to be seen as particularly grave, profound and lasting in their impact on victims (Davis 2005). Moreover, as the adult psyche is understood as rooted in childhood (Lawler 2000), any psychological consequences of sexual crimes against children can be seen as endless and even irreversible. Taking this further, the discourse of violence incorporates the idea that paedophiles do not just traumatise children but destroy them. This 'destruction' is variously referred to as a destruction of childhood:

> Jack: They're a child, and, their **innocence** has been lost, not really lost, it's been **taken away** from them.

> Beth: He [paedophile] **robbed** her [victim] of her **childhood**.. it was just.. **butchered**. [Beth]

or as a destruction of life:

Many victims of abuse had their **lives destroyed**. (J. Joyce, 'Sex and sin', *Guardian* 17 August 2000, p. 19)

Beth: It's ruined, they've [paedophiles] **wrecked** a child's **life**.

Sarah: You're taking that kid's life, it's still alive but you're **taking** that kid's **life away**.

This destruction of life is usually not real, in the sense of causing death, but metaphorical. It is the destruction of a concept, childhood, and its defining element of innocence. Symbolic and real 'destruction' can be conflated because the discourse of innocence facilitates equations of children's lives and childhood with asexuality (see Chapter 2).

Phoenix and Oerton (2005) note that adult victims of rape or serious sexual assault are constructed as undergoing social death. This social death refers to an individual's inability to act as a full social actor, and is constructed through a totalising victim narrative according to which the trauma of violation affects the very person. Consequently, the victim's autonomy and agency, their ability to function as full social actors, are seriously doubted. Popular conceptions of the sexual violation of children and adults (women) are similar in that both pronounce the death and destruction of the victim. But in contrast to rape portrayals, the child sexual abuse discourse focuses on the death of a *concept* and derives from this the death of the *person*: children are pronounced dead because their childhood has been destroyed. The idea of the death of child*hood* and its logically preceding position is arguably needed to mobilise the totalising victim narrative. Children in contemporary society are conceptualised as lacking a range of adult skills, experiences and knowledge; hence they are not perceived as full social actors (Qvortrup 2005) and it becomes difficult to conceptualise them as undergoing social death (in the sense of caused by a loss of agency). The concept of the death of childhood makes this possible because the death of child*ren* can be claimed on the basis of – and via equations with – the death of child*hood*.

Generally speaking, the discourse of violence is popular; it is frequently used in the media and focus groups to understand and portray paedophiles. By attributing violence and aggression as typical characteristics, it categorises and demonises paedophiles, especially as their violence is understood as cruel and intentional. However, this general trend is complicated by different frequencies of deployment of the discourse of violence. The *Guardian* does not use and reproduce the discourse of violence as much as the *NOTW*, and the second focus group did not use it at all, suggesting a mix of media power. The media possess the power to disseminate ways of thinking about paedophilia; some participants have even adopted certain discursive constructs such as 'the destruction of childhood' and related soundbites ('he robbed her of her childhood'). Yet there are limits to media power, as one group ignores the discourse of violence. This is most likely to be an active decision rather than ignorance because of the high level of exposure to such media ideas. If this is the case then there are opportunities for individuals to reject aspects of the discursive framework, and to an extent remain outside it.

Cunning

The discourse of the cunning paedophile is pervasive in both the *NOTW* and the *Guardian*. It constructs paedophiles as meticulously and carefully planning their actions and seeking out children, as very smart, clever and difficult to catch. Like the discourses of evil, perversion/pathology and violence, it categorises and others paedophiles by defining certain characteristics as typical of a social group. However, it is not as easily demonising. While cunning is not an attribute with positive connotations, it restores human-ness (i.e. being human but not humane, kind) to 'the paedophile' by being a distinctly human, rational, thinking form of behaviour. The discourse exists in a great variety of aspects and is often constructed through stories on how planning, calculating and strategic paedophiles are. For example, paedophiles are said to plan every detail of their crimes, create opportunities for abuse or take on new identities:

> Pervert James McAlpine, 34, attacked several boys after **reinventing** himself on his release from jail in 1998 after serving 30 months. He **evaded detection** when applying for a job as a **kids' tennis coach** because he had legally **changed his name**, despite his sex offences. (M. Jones, 'Plug this loophole', *NOTW* 8 September 2002, p. 8)

The strategic, methodical nature of behaviour is constructed not only through stories (events and actions) but also through some key lexical items which strongly encourage interpretation of these actions and events as cunning, e.g. 'evade' or 'reinvent'. Further, the discourse of cunning involves a dimension of slyness, shrewdness, manipulation and deceit. This dimension is conveyed through words such as 'lure', 'entice' or 'trick':

> Police forces and a social services department were facing accusations that their blunders let the former school caretaker gain a **position** which he used to **lure** the 10-year-olds into his house. (S. Morris et al., 'Blunder after blunder', *Guardian* 18 December 2003, p. 1)

These words suggest that the agent, 'the paedophile', has manipulated, misled and deceived the object, children, by tempting and coaxing them into certain actions through false promises and pretences:

> Hertfordshire: Whereabouts unknown: Peter McKenzie, 49. Released early after being jailed for 15 years in 1989 for **tricking** girls aged six and seven into sexual intercourse with **promises of magical powers**. ('Evil that preys on our children', *NOTW* 30 July 2000, pp. 4–5)

Cunning behaviour is distinctly human, rational and cognitive, and in contrast to Cohen's (1972) concept of the folk devil, paedophiles are not simply portrayed as thoroughly devilish or inhuman. To miss their human-ness is to miss what makes paedophiles so dangerous: their human appearance and ways of acting, as well as their human skills and capabilities which are needed for thinking strategically or acting deceitfully. If 'the paedophile' was simply an evil monster then he or she would not possess such skills and could be easily identified, detected and combated. 'The paedophile' is conceptualised as looking and acting human, and these two aspects are preconditions which enable him or her to obtain jobs and interact with other adults and children. The discourses of evil and cunning are in some ways juxtaposed. Evil suggests demonic-ness, inhumanity and irrationality, while cunning connotes human-ness, extreme rationality and thought.

Through these opposing discourses 'the paedophile', like several gothic monsters, is constructed as possessing a dual identity. It is portrayed as appearing normal as human on the outside, and a malicious devil on the inside (Jancovich 1992):

> Beneath the **respectable façade** that Huntley **presented** to the school interview panel **lurked** a man with a proclivity for very young women and girls and a willingness to use **violence** when denied. (S. Morris, 'His lies and shallow charm fooled dozens of people but they **hid** a violent, bitter man', *Guardian* 18 December 2003, p. 3)

The inner evil is seen as the true identity, as the core which is hidden behind a performance. Words such as 'façade' indicate this clearly. Dual identity, which amounts to a 'monster within' or 'invisible monstrosity', makes 'the paedophile' particularly dangerous because it destroys any opportunity for 'us' to detect danger visually and protect ourselves, as we do not know who and where danger is. 'The paedophile' is in that sense invisible and the flipside is that anyone could be a paedophile. Further, human qualities such as rationality and thinking endow 'the paedophile' with considerable skills and power which, in conjunction with evil, reinforce the danger. These constructions are central to the incitement of fear; the danger of the figure of 'the paedophile' lies in its ambiguous and dual identity rather than simple negativity (Cohen 1972) or humanness (Collier 2001). When the *NOTW* demands public access to the sex offender register, i.e. to specific visual, personal and spatial information about paedophiles, then these demands are justified by enabling the public to identify specific paedophiles visually. The monster is not killed but defeated by making its inner, invisible monstrosity visible, which robs it of its danger and power. This is central to the common-sense appeal of community notification.

Space

The discourse of the cunning paedophile is produced through three strategies which paedophiles are said to devise and carry out in order to create opportunities for abuse: space, 'grooming' and employment (getting jobs involving children). The strategy of space proposes that paedophiles strategically hang out in typical children's places in order to find children to abuse sexually. Common examples include parks, playgrounds, funfairs and swimming baths:

> He [Roy Whiting] moved into a flat a short walk from the Harbour Park **amusement park**, a **children's playground**, and the shingle **beach**. [. . .] There is no direct evidence Whiting began **hunting** for children but the alibi he gave for his movements on the day of Sarah's murder may be telling. He claimed he sat in two **parks** and went to a **fair**. Detectives believe he came up with these locations because they were the places he did often visit. Two and a half years after leaving prison . . . Whiting was again to be found near where children were playing, apparently waiting for his chance to **pounce**. (S. Morris, 'How an eight-year-old **misfit** became a notorious killer', 13 December 2001, p. 3)

A PAEDOPHILE . . . Peter Lander-Jones, 63, was jailed in July for breaching a lifetime sex offender order which bars him from speaking to under-18s and entering **youth haunts** including **parks, swimming pools** and **playgrounds.** ('Euro law may help sex beast', *NOTW* 27 August 2000, p. 17)

In all focus groups participants widely reproduced the discourse of the cunning paedophile as strategically seeking out popular children's places, and they used the same examples as the media:

A. M.: So do you think there are any places that are particularly dangerous for children?
Beth: Parks.
Pat: Swimming baths.. well, anywhere where there's children.
Sarah: They got the other playground but.. you used to get the old men, sitting there on the benches watching the little kids!
Sinead: Even schools though, you get them there!

Importantly, media discourses possess the power to shape practices as some parents will no longer leave their children unsupervised in public places, especially not in those considered typical 'paedophile places', such as parks, playgrounds or around schools (see the section on parental governance in chapter 5). Nevertheless, the media are not immune from critique, and one participant challenged the idea of paedophiles frequenting children's places:

A. M.: Are there any particularly dangerous places for children?
Jack: Playgrounds, funfairs, seasides.
James: I disagree with all that though, to be fair . . . Cause that's just what they say in the papers.

James's dismissal of this discursive idea as media mythmaking illustrates that a discourse can always be challenged by individuals, no matter how widely accepted it is. Participants have an ambiguous relationship to the media in that the latter are seen as both reflecting reality and truth, and fabricating stories. This parallels the ambiguous relationship the media have to themselves. Broadsheets for instance have taken on the concept of a moral panic to criticise the actions of tabloids as manufacturing fear, while being implicated in this process themselves.

The *NOTW*'s actions in the case of paedophilia illustrate how and why broadsheets can make such claims. The *NOTW* wants to provide images of cunning, 'grooming' behaviour but real

2 *News of the World*, 25 August 2002

photographs of paedophiles hanging out in children's places are not available. As a result, the *NOTW* resorts to producing such images with models. For example, on 25 August 2002 the *NOTW*'s article 'Evil monsters in our midst – hidden by the law' was illustrated with an A4-size photograph showing an adult male behind the fence of a playground watching children play. On 16 November 2003 the article 'Tory peers bid to wreck Sarah's Law' was accompanied by a large photograph of an adult male walking in a park, holding the hand of a female child. Both photographs are taken from the back, creating the impression that the respective adult male is in control, either by occupying an observing position or by showing the adult as leading the child away.

The impact of these photographs goes beyond illustrating texts and discourses. In our culture visual images, especially photographs, have a particular importance in being seen as factual and establishing the truth (Graddol 1994). In that sense they 'prove' to readers that this form of behaviour really exists and forms a characteristic of paedophiles. In the bottom right-hand corners of both pictures it is acknowledged that these photographs involve models, but this is unlikely to diminish their impact. First, photographs overwhelm writings through their enormously larger sizes. Second, compared to the linguistic the visual possesses a density which makes it more prominent and arresting (Jordanova 2000). Third, the bottom right-hand corner is the least salient part of the asymmetrical visual field and therefore unlikely to gain the reader's gaze and attention (Kress and Van Leeuwen 1996). In the first photograph the *NOTW* even directly pre-empts any challenge to the truth status of images by stating that they may not be a document of a real situation but are certainly representative of reality: 'DANGER LURKS: Paedophiles operate under a cloak of anonymity. Our picture is posed by models. The reality is terrifying.' To construct photographs deliberately to fit discursive descriptions and claims is extraordinary, extremely sensationalist, and can be accused of 'manufacturing fear'. It is not surprising that the *Guardian*, even though it produces the idea of 'the paedophile' frequenting children's places, does not engage in this strategy. This kind of journalistic practice is in danger of losing credibility and respectability by overtly manipulating reality, and forms a basis on which broadsheets can accuse the tabloid press of manufacturing fears and moral panics, while exempting themselves from these processes.

Posed by models

3 *News of the World*, 16 November 2003

'Grooming'

If the first strategy has illustrated the power of the media to disseminate its ideas widely, the concept of 'grooming' produces quite different results. 'Grooming' refers to a process in which paedophiles are said to befriend children and gain their trust in order to get close to and abuse them (Lumby 1997). This is a specific and popular way to produce 'the paedophile' as cunning:

> Patrick Green . . . logged on to a chatroom called Younger Girls for Older Men and exchanged messages with the girl for two months, **gaining** her **trust** before arranging a meeting and then abusing her. [. . .] Green then arranged a series of secret meetings by **flattering** the teenager via the chatroom. (A. Chrisafis, '5 years for man who **lured** girl via internet', *Guardian* 25 October 2000, p. 7)

> Carol Downie, 48, revealed how Victor Burnett had been trying to **'befriend'** two of her boys and other children from the troubled Paulsgrove district in Portsmouth. . . . When he [Burnett] moved to Paulsgrove local parents were kept in the dark about his past, leaving him free to forge **friendships** with **youngsters**. ('Mum thanks us for rescuing her sons', *NOTW* 13 August 2000, p. 5)

The *NOTW* and the *Guardian* widely understand paedophiles as employing a strategy of 'grooming'. Even if the *Guardian* sometimes puts the term 'groom' in quotation marks and thereby questions it, most articles and journalists remain committed to the basic aspects of the process as a reality.

Focus group participants who do express opinions about 'grooming' hold the same conceptions as the two newspapers. Being nice to children is presented as the way in which 'grooming' is carried out:

> Fiona: Somebody pays them [children] a bit of love and attention . . .
> they're gonna think, like, somebody's being *nice* to them, you know.

Examples of the strategy of 'being nice' include flattering children, playing with children, offering them presents, and even owning a pet as a useful tool in the 'grooming' process:

> Lisa: And he's [local paedophile] got this little dog with him, he used to say to the kids 'Come and look at it!'
> Pat: The kids used to go round to the little dog.. that's probably why he had the dog.
> Claire: Yeah, **to attract children**.

However, the idea of 'grooming' does not emerge at all in two out of three groups, despite its popularity with the media. There are no obvious reasons why a discursive concept should be so popular with one focus group and not with two others, especially when the latter two have accepted the general discourse of the cunning paedophile. This absence is even more remarkable in the context of the concept of 'grooming' having become part of the official language and government legislation (e.g. Sexual Offences Act 2003). While this focus group study was too small to offer representative explanations for inter-group variations, its findings emphasise the need for research into the attitudes and discursive understandings of the wider public. Their conceptions and opinions cannot simply be read off from the discourses and attitudes of institutions like the media or the law.

Employment

The discourse of the cunning paedophile is further produced through the idea that paedophiles actively seek out jobs involving children with the aim of creating opportunities of abuse. As a consequence of paedophiles obtaining certain jobs, certain institutions are seen as systematically infiltrated by individual paedophiles or paedophile rings. Both the *NOTW* and the *Guardian* understand paedophiles as engaged in a strategy of employment but vary in terms of examples. While the *Guardian* focuses on the Catholic church, care-home and childcare professions, and education, the *NOTW* focuses on scout leaders, teachers, babysitters and sports coaches:

> North London: Brent: Robert Tickner, 39. Deputy **headmaster** jailed for four years in 1990 for molesting four boys, age 11 to 16, at Woodfield School. [. . .]
>
> North Yorks: Skipton: David Hope. **Choirmaster** jailed for 20 months in 1996 for sexually assaulting pupils at the **boarding school** where he taught. [. . .]
>
> Stirlingshire: New Culloden: John Tonner, 48. **PE teacher** jailed for a year in 1999 for abusing two teenage boys during weights-training sessions. [. . .]
>
> Allan Ewan, Methven, near Perth: 47. **Ex-Scout master** jailed for 15 months in 1998 for sex offences against youths between 15 and 18. (T. Taras and P. McMullan, 'Does a monster live near you?', *NOTW* 23 July 2000, pp. 2–3)

Through the multiplicity and repeated coverage of single case stories – which are seen as representing real life – both the *NOTW* and the *Guardian* not only produce 'the paedophile' as a cunning figure but foster the impression of a pattern of systematic infiltration of certain professions. These claims can also be made more directly, in which case the *Guardian* often attributes them to respectable claims-makers. Quoting authority figures such as public inquiry leaders lends status and truth value to claims:

> The man who led the public inquiry into 20 years of abuse in **children's homes** in north Wales last night warned that abusers could have **infiltrated** the **foster care system** and could now prove even harder to detect. (D. Brindle, 'Foster care system "at risk from abusers"', *Guardian* 17 February 2000, p. 11)

Further, both newspapers emphasise the intentional and deliberate nature of the process of paedophiles obtaining certain jobs:

> The **boy scout movement,** aware it has long been a **target** for sexual predators, has amassed the most complete list of child sex offenders in Britain. [. . .] **Five in every 1000 applications are singled out as having more sinister intentions and barred.** ('Scouting out the beasts', *NOTW* 23 July 2000, p. 5)

Words and expressions such as 'target', 'infiltrate' or 'latest scandal' in particular suggest that incidents are not one-offs but deliberate and parts of a pattern:

> The Roman Catholic archbishop of Cardiff yesterday issued an apology and agreed to be replaced following the **latest scandal** concerning **paedophile priests** in his diocese. (S. Bates, 'Archbishop steps aside in paedophile scandal', *Guardian* 6 November 2000, p. 8)

Neologisms like 'paedophile priest' have become part of the vocabulary and help reinforce the link between the church and paedophiles in the popular mind by providing a condensed representation for it. The *Guardian*'s critical attitude towards religion, and towards the Catholic church with its conservative teachings in particular, seems to shape its interest in and particular coverage of the topic.

Many of the common examples used within this discourse – teachers, care professionals, priests etc. – concern jobs commonly classed as respectable, professional and possessing social status, thereby making social class and related notions of respectability central themes. Paedophiles are fundamentally unrespectable, valueless and lacking any social status, making it difficult for people to reconcile images of 'the paedophile' and the 'middle-class professional'. This difficulty expresses itself in focus group discussions in exclamations of disbelief and surprise:

> Fiona: What about people who work like in children's homes that are supposed to have respectable jobs and that.
> Donna: Oh yeah, and policemen and judges!

While focus group participants widely understand paedophiles as cunning people gaining employment involving children, this understanding is mediated by personal experiences and circumstances. These factors influence memory of and concern with a discourse, and therefore arguably mediate the media's power to shape understanding and practices. For example, two participants, Ellie and Celia, need full-time professional childcare due to work commitments and the age of their children. Consequently, they are particularly worried about paedophiles infiltrating childcare professions. All participants in the first group are interested in 'paedophile teachers' because they are training to be teachers. Mediation through personal circumstances can therefore reinforce the impact of discourses. Being personally concerned correlates with being interested in media discourses, remembering them and adjusting practices in their light.

The connections between media impact and personal positions are, however, complicated in two ways. First, personal circumstances may encourage interest in yet disbelief of media discourses. For instance, trainee teachers reacted to media reports on teachers sexually abusing children with some disbelief:

> Kerry: And that female teacher that, from Canada, that was having sex with them fifteen-year-old lads.. cause I mean **you would've thought** that they're safe, that your kids would be **safe with a teacher** wouldn't you.

This disbelief is probably due to the 'respectable' nature of teaching as an occupation, and the traditional image of teachers as protectors. Trainee teachers have already internalised this image and adopted the subject position of a teacher:

> Jack: You know, at the end of the day, we're gonna be teachers so we've got to protect the kids.

Hence, the second complicating factor concerns multiple and contradictory positioning (Davies and Harré 2001). Individuals tend to occupy more than one position, for instance participants in group 1 occupy the positions of 'parent' and 'future teacher', and are part of the 'normal majority' which is juxtaposed to paedophiles. If the media position individuals in incongruent ways they can foster doubt and rejection of certain discourses. As parents and part of the 'normal majority', participants in group 1 are positioned as moral protectors and 'non-paedophiles'. Yet as trainee teachers the discourse of cunning positions them as individuals who are more likely to be paedophiles than other professionals. Contradictory positioning results in an ambivalent relationship of individuals to media discourses, marked by a mix of acceptance and disbelief.

The strategies of space and employment add a spatial dimension to the figure of 'the paedophile' and its ambiguity. Simmel (1971) has argued that the stranger is not simply someone unknown but rather produced through a synthesis of remoteness and closeness. He or she is an outsider within. Closeness is rooted in the facts that the stranger is spatially close (shares the space of a social group) and shares general qualities and characteristics with other members of the group, e.g. nationality or human nature. The stranger is remote in the sense of not possessing the specific qualities and characteristics common to the group he or she lives with, such as particular customs, practices and views. From this perspective, 'the paedophile' elicits such fear because of the synthesis of closeness and remoteness. The figure of 'the paedophile' stranger is close in the sense that he or she shares 'our' social spaces (e.g. parks, schools, playgrounds) and social circles (e.g. as priests, teachers, childminders or football coaches). But the discursive figure of 'the paedophile' is also remote in Simmel's sense of being a person who is not personally close to us (e.g. friends or family members are excluded by the discourse of stranger danger) and in supposedly not sharing contemporary society's particular codes and conventions of (sexual) behaviour, such as the 'taboo' of sexual interest in children. This helps explain the tensions and fears which the figure of 'the paedophile' is able to raise. If it was simply remote, e.g. by not inhabiting our social spaces and circles, then it would not be an immediate danger and fears could be contained more easily. Similarly, if 'the paedophile' was simply close, e.g. a friend, family member or community member, then a (false) sense of knowledge and trust would keep danger at bay. Thus it is the synthesis of remoteness and closeness, the essence of the stranger, which makes the paedophile figure so dangerous. It is elusive yet threatens to be present in particular spaces, profession and disguises:

> Hannah: I get more nervous in areas where that, where there are children's areas.. cause as far as I'm concerned.. a paedophile is gonna be where children are.. so.

Categorisation versus individualisation

The *NOTW* and the *Guardian* use the same discourses to construct 'the paedophile' as a discursive figure; however, they vary in terms of frequency, stereotyping, preferred choice and sensational terminology. Therefore the kind of figure created is not identical, e.g. 'the paedophile' in the *NOTW* emerges as more violent, evil and perverted than in the *Guardian*, yet it is similar in that it is constructed through the same basic discourses. Further, both the media and people in this study are very much involved in the typification and categorisation of paedophiles. Categorisation details a portrayal of paedophiles as generally knowable through the ascription of certain psychological and behavioural features.

Protection guides, which the *NOTW* occasionally offers, amount to a summary of some of these features:

> EVERY parent in Britain needs to know how to spot a paedophile – and this cut-out-and-keep guide will help them. [. . .]
>
> WHO ARE THE PAEDOPHILES?
> They can be found in all professions, all levels of society, be from any race or religion and can be a friend, relative or acquaintance. . . . Paedophiles often come across as 'nice **men**' which helps them to get close to parents and their children. They are attracted to places and jobs offering easy access to kids. [. . .]
>
> HOW DO THEY OPERATE?
> Paedophiles are often well organised, manipulative and sophisticated at attaching themselves to families. They often befriend hard-pressed parents facing difficulties. . . . Paedophiles may offer money, babysitting and emotional support or start a relationship with a parent to move into the home. They often try to win over a child with gifts, outings and holidays. [. . .]

HOW TO SPOT A PAEDOPHILE
Be alert to **any adult** who pays an unusual amount of attention to your child. . . . Question why **any adult** is seeking to be alone with your child. ('How to protect your children', *NOTW* 6 August 2000, p. 4)

Protection guides entail the *NOTW* telling parents how to identify and recognise paedophiles by describing typical characteristics (e.g. organised, manipulative) and specific behaviour patterns (e.g. attracted to places and jobs offering easy access to kids, 'grooming'). This categorises and others paedophiles semantically, assuming and claiming that paedophiles are a knowable and recognisable type of person. Moreover, paedophiles are grammatically othered as they are referred to through the personal pronoun 'they', which denotes a group of people not including the speaker or the reader, and connotes the 'Other' (Fairclough 1989).

Collier (2001) has noted that paedophiles are portrayed as both insiders and outsiders, as 'Other' and part of society, as knowable and unknowable. This last dichotomy is for Collier grounded in the difference between the paedo*phile* and paedo*philia*, the former being identifiable while the latter remains elusive. While this is true, the dichotomy or double portrayal is also grounded in the figure of 'the paedophile' itself which is both identifiable and elusive. While engaged in a process of categorisation which portrays paedophiles as knowable, the media simultaneously claim that anyone could be a paedophile ('any adult'), suggesting that paedophiles can*not* be known or identified. This is a process of universalisation–individualisation in the sense that paedophiles are conceptualised as individuals and potentially *any* individual. Thus I do not want to argue that Bell's (2002) claim that paedophiles are constructed as unknowable individuals is incorrect; indeed the *NOTW* has greatly popularised and exploited this idea to justify its demand for public access to the sex offender register. Parents have been portrayed as needing *specific* information in order to identify individual paedophiles and protect their children effectively. However, Bell, like moral panic theorists, only acknowledges one side of media practices, and this might be grounded in too 'rational' an approach to the media. The two processes of categorisation and universalisation–individualisation, and their respective claims that paedophiles are an identifiable type and an unknowable individual ('anyone'), are contradictory and logically mutually exclusive. However, that does not stop the media from

supporting and constructing both. And again, the danger potential
of 'the paedophile' lies in exactly this contradiction: the media construct 'the paedophile' as a highly dangerous type while universalising this type, locating it in potentially anyone.

Recognition: the figure of 'the paedophile', stranger danger and gender

In focus groups many participants expressed the same contradictory
views as the media. On the one hand, they claimed that anyone
could be a paedophile, i.e. that paedophiles are unknowable and
unrecognisable:

> Amy: I don't think you can distinguish between a paedophile and.. a
> non-paedophile, you just can't.
> Sarah: Could be anyone really . . . anyone.

Community notification is demanded on the basis of specific knowledge enabling them to recognise particular paedophiles, and protect
their children by avoiding specific individuals:

> Sarah: I'd like to know about.. whether they [paedophiles] live in the
> area.
> Donna: You should tell your kids 'Never go to that house, stay away
> from that man!'
> Fiona: At least you can point them out to your children then, couldn't
> you so.
> Beth: Yeah, 'He's a paedophile, don't go near him, don't talk to him,
> don't.. look at him!' . . . Cause then at least you give your kids a
> chance, aren't you, to let them know.

On the other hand, participants also and contradictorily believe
that paedophiles are recognisable and that you can protect yourself
through recognition:

> Beth: You know like your mum didn't say: 'Right, when you go to the
> park watch out for the paedophile!', like *we* do *today*.

> Ellie: But in places like parks then.. I might look around and see who's
> there.

If paedophiles were not a recognisable category, then there would
be no one and nothing for participants to watch out for, or tell their
children to watch out for. At stake is clearly the specificity of knowledge and information. Participants do believe that paedophiles can

be identified through some general characteristics typical of this group of people, which are exemplified by the discursive figure of 'the paedophile', and in the absence of community notification they rely on this general knowledge.

Phoenix and Oerton (2005) have argued that the child sex offender is constituted as unknowable through recent legislation which extends to anyone who comes into any contact with a child. Hence, any (adult) person as well as any situation, interaction or relation involving adults and children is treated as suspicious and needing regulation. The new law against grooming illustrates this argument forcefully as it allows for interpreting *any* interaction or contact with a child as having possible sexual intentions. However, the grooming law itself is also an instance where the law knows 'the paedophile' in the sense that it is based on a behaviour pattern said to be typical of 'the paedophile'. Child sexual abuse is a very wide category which seems unknowable because no one is ever quite sure which behaviours to include or exclude, but the figure of 'the paedophile' remains a specific type with a fairly narrow range of activities which are seen as *definitely* constituting abuse. Further, at least from this focus group research it is clear that in practice (some) members of the public do treat paedophiles as to some extent knowable, and only suspect those individuals who conform to the figure of 'the paedophile'.

The same kind of complexity and contradiction repeats itself with regards to gender. Participants watch out for strangers and men only:

A. M.: How do you spot a paedophile then?
Kerry: Old men.
Miles: Man.
Kerry: Yeah, a man.
Amy: Yeah, you do immediately think of a man when you think of paedophiles.
Jack: You do.

Similarly, the *NOTW* simply assumed in its protection guide above that paedophiles are male, so readers are not told to beware anyone but to beware any male (stranger). Paedophiles are *strange men* who seek out employment with children, and befriend parents and/or children previously unknown to them through various measures (e.g. 'Paedophiles often come across as "nice **men**" ').

Further, many of the characteristics attributed to 'the paedophile' only make sense if paedophiles are equated with strangers, e.g. the discourse of the cunning paedophile only works if we assume that paedophiles, as strangers, have to get access to children they do not already know. In this sense stranger danger underlies paedophilia stories, and implicated in the discourse of stranger danger is a construction of parents and familiar people as safe (Ahmed 2000). This is often latent but in protection guides parents are obviously positioned as protectors of children. It *is* mentioned in the *NOTW*'s article that paedophiles do not have to be strangers, but 'can be a friend, relative or acquaintance'. However, this single-sentence statement is overwhelmed by a set-up which presumes and reinforces stranger danger. This is a good example of how the media generally deal with the issue. There is episodic recognition that most child sexual abuse happens in families (La Fontaine 1990), but this is overpowered by a continuous discourse of stranger danger. As far are numbers are concerned, a media review by Kitzinger and Skidmore (1995) has shown that 96 per cent of newspaper articles relating to the protection of children are concerned with threats from strangers (Kitzinger 2004).

The figure of 'the paedophile' therefore operates as a guide on the basis of two fundamental framework characteristics: stranger-ness and gender (maleness). As these two characteristics are visual they can be quickly assessed, and if they are not present the processes of recognition and suspicion do not even begin. Focus group participants only ever suspected male strangers of being paedophiles, suggesting that 'the paedophile' is not simply degendered (Cowburn and Dominelli 2001) or that official discourses on sexual offences against adults and children have not simply become gender neutral (Phoenix and Oerton 2005). Rather the figure is represented as male, as Collier (2001) suggests, but maleness is taken for granted. Gender in this sense is neither simply present nor absent but simultaneously present *and* absent; it is present in constant assumptions and absent in that it is not recognised as an issue. Consequently there is no idea that masculinity might be important in understanding why male adults sexually abuse children. Pathology, not masculinity, is the key to explanations. For this reason I disagree with Collier's (2001) interpretation of paedophilia as involving an (active) recognition of crime and danger as masculine phenomena and, consequently, as disturbing men's location within the social per se. Explanations for patterns of absence and presence cannot simply be sought in the individualisation of a social problem. Maleness and masculinity are individual as well as social-context factors, and could feature much more prominently in paedophilia controversies. Yet while 'the paedophile' is widely represented as male, maleness and masculinity are not seen as a cause for comment or analysis. Also, representations of maleness are more inconspicuous and automatic than other discursive characteristics producing the figure of 'the paedophile'. Maleness, like stranger-ness, is so ingrained that it is both overrepresented and beyond (explicit) representation, constantly present yet absent (Ahmed 2000).

When participants watch out for (male) strangers, not all strangers are suspected as paedophiles or are recognised as dangerous. Some strangers are recognised as stranger and more dangerous than others (Ahmed 2000), and the decisive factor is the figure of 'the paedophile' and its characteristics. Focus group participants suspect only those strangers of being paedophiles who display behavioural characteristics which are commonly described as typical of paedophiles, such as devoting attention to children:

> Fiona: Every **man** . . . that might pay any attention to your children. . . . I do still have this feeling of like 'You might be a sweet man but actually.. why are you paying so much attention to my child?'

or men offering presents to children:

> Donna: But listen, when we went to Halifax . . . and the little one in the pram, and this little old **man** came over and looked and went 'Ahh' and gave him a little toy. . . . He looked at him and what did he want?

Both forms of behaviour conform to the concepts of cunning and 'grooming', and so does being present in a children's place without any apparent purpose (such as being with a child):

> Lisa: Can you remember when we were in Halifax.. that museum thing . . . that **fella** there, and I said to Alice.. 'He could be a paedophile.'
> Donna: Come looking at the kids.
> Fiona: But his kids came out then, didn't they.
> Lisa: He **could have** been a paedophile.

Some commentators have interpreted the child sexual abuse controversy as leading to a reconfiguration of the child from subject to object of sexual desire, with the consequence that everyone, but especially the parent, is seen as a potential sexual abuser (Bauman 1997). However, this analysis suggests otherwise. Parents are sometimes thought of as putting their children *at* risk but not as being *a* risk, a paedophile. The above anecdote from a group excursion reveals that several members of one focus group suspected a museum visitor of being a paedophile, yet they changed their minds when the suspect met his children, parenthood seemingly precluding being a paedophile.

In the processes of recognition the mode of recognition is partly visual, based on visible social characteristics such as gender and stranger-ness. But as the contemporary figure of 'the paedophile' is constructed through psychological and behavioural rather than appearance characteristics, recognition is strongly guided by the character mapping of this figure. From a risk perspective not all strangers are identified as risky; the existence of risks is knowledge-dependent and necessarily mediated (Beck 2000). We have to know about risks to be aware of them *as* risks, and the figure of 'the paedophile' is central to this knowledge.

Figures and fears

Claiming paedophiles as simultaneously knowable and unknowable, a type and an individual (anyone), devil and human is precisely what makes them so dangerous. Constructing paedophiles around these binaries means that a figure emerges which is devilish and potentially anyone. As Kincaid (1998: 74) points out, 'while we maintain the monstrous and perverse criminality of the act, we also make it universal and inevitable'. However, these claims are clearly contradictory. How can 'the paedophile' be different and possess typical characteristics, yet also be universal? How can paedophiles be distinct devils, yet unidentifiable humans? How can paedophiles be driven by irrational evil and perversion, yet be so controlled as to plan their actions and exercise them with care?

These contradictions are made viable as constructions of the figure of 'the paedophile' tap into wider cultural resources and our cultural heritage. Drawing on gothic narratives and their figures makes such contradictions appear less unusual. For example, the dual identity theme is the essence of gothic monsters such as the werewolf, and has been a feature of many cultural artefacts. *Jekyll and Hyde* is a famous literary example. This generally entrenches the idea that identities can have different and contradictory facets, even though one facet tends to be seen as the real one deeply hidden by a shallow appearance. Further, while 'the paedophile' as described in this chapter is very much a figure of our times, it has a general predecessor in the dangerous stranger giving sweets to children. Children in North American and European countries at least have been warned for decades not to talk to strangers and not to accept sweets, or other presents, from strangers even though they may seem nice and friendly. Again, the niceness is seen as a front for malicious intentions and badness underneath. The contemporary figure of 'the paedophile' is much more detailed than this, but its essence and contradictions are aspects of wider cultural figures and ideas.

The contradictions of the figure of 'the paedophile' are also rendered less visible through a particular use of ideas on morality and cognition. For example, the discourse of evil contains terminology which likens paedophiles to animals, and serves to exclude them from the category of humanity. However, this animal analogy is used selectively as only some animal qualities are transferred onto paedophiles. On the one hand, animal behaviour is usually understood to be violent, instinct-driven and without conscience, and these qualities are attributed to paedophiles. On the other hand, animal behaviour also tends to be understood as unconscious and carried out without thinking, but these qualities are not attributed to paedophiles. On the contrary, the ideas of the cunning, prepared and well-organised paedophile suggest a high degree of rationality and awareness. Paedophiles are portrayed not as accidental but as cruel criminals who are fully aware of the implications of their actions, and engage in them despite this knowledge. Through the discourses of evil, violence and cunning, and the selective use of the animal analogy, a truly menacing and terrifying type of person is constructed: irrational, instinct-driven, violent, evil and without conscience like an animal, yet cunning, organised, manipulative and planning like a very rational, intelligent human being. Cognitively paedophiles are constructed as very much human, yet morally as subhuman, evil and without conscience.

The fascination with evil figures goes some way towards explaining concern and fear. The media produce a truly terrifying figure and universalise it, maintaining that anyone could be this figure. While this dangerous figure may be able to incite interest and fear there are central questions left unanswered. Our culture and society are obviously involved in the creation of paedophiles as dangerous demons and in fights against them (Kincaid 1998); but why should we want to do that? What is the gain? Further, it is not obvious why 'the paedophile' rather than some other figure should be constructed in this way. The gothic narrative approach is based on the assumption that constant debates and actions on paedophilia are not engaged in for the sake of children because there are many other pressing issues affecting children. Moreover, media interest in child sexual abuse is episodic, driven by events, rather than genuine and consistent. For example, convicted child sex offenders were banned from travelling to South East Asia following the tsunami disaster in 2004, but male sex tourism, much of it aimed at the underage, to the same region is usually tolerated (O'Connell Davidson 1995). Debates around paedophilia may simply reflect the fact that adult society is interested in this topic and gets something out of talking about it (Kincaid 1998). The question is what this 'something' is.

Some disease theorists (e.g. Gilman 1988) have argued that the diseased are represented as inherently different 'Others' in order to manage societal anxiety about disease by locating and controlling it. We construct strict boundaries between 'them' and 'us' in an attempt to contain fears of being at risk by projecting it onto certain 'Others'. By implication, we do not want to entertain the idea that the diseased are very much like us in many respects because it makes the world ambiguous, terrifying and dangerous. However, this does not quite fit constructions around paedophilia. The construction of 'the paedophile' as a dangerous figure is based on major binary oppositions. 'The paedophile' is simultaneously seen as quite 'normal', like 'us', human in many aspects of his or her life *and* as totally different and 'other'. This suggests that while the construction of boundaries between 'us' and the 'Other' might serve our desire for security and certainty, we are also prone to fuel our own fears and anxieties by producing an ambiguous figure which cannot easily be othered and contained. We need to explain the contradictory function of creating both security and anxiety, which is reflected in the similarly ambiguous relation to outrage and disgust. On the one hand society abhors what paedophiles do; on the other hand it is fascinated by it and feeds its own fascinations through very detailed reports on it.

From a gothic narratives perspective people are fascinated by monsters and find pleasure in emotions traditionally considered negative, such as fear, horror and anxiety, at least when experienced as induced by fictional forms. This is why horror films or gothic novels have such an appeal; the audience enjoys the stimulation of these emotions. From this point of view we can see the preoccupation with paedophilia, based on the construction of 'the paedophile' as a highly dangerous figure, as grounded in society enjoying the shock, horror and anxiety that these stories produce. However, the paedophilia story is also about othering paedophiles, i.e. achieving security. Stimulating anxiety, through constructions of 'the paedophile' as human and dangerous, may be pleasurable as long as anxieties are somewhat contained through categorisation and othering. These controversial interpretations do not explain why paedophiles in particular have become the subject of such interest and constructions, yet they might explain why the incestuous father has not become the figurative embodiment of child sexual abuse. As a figure well integrated in social life (husband, father, friend etc.) he is much more difficult to other and demonise than the stranger paedophile. As a consequence, danger could *genuinely* be located in anyone and anywhere, and anxiety could not be contained and counteracted. This suggests and presumes that the stimulation of anxiety is only pleasurable as long as it is somehow limited, either by being invoked through fiction or by ideas of the recognisable 'Other'. From this perspective media and popular contradictions in the construction of paedophiles make sense by serving to stimulate yet contain anxieties.

Conclusions

This chapter has outlined the major discourses and concepts around paedophilia, and argued that through them certain psycho-social and behavioural characteristics are attributed as typical to paedophiles. This process of categorisation produces 'the paedophile' as a detailed discursive figure. While both the *Guardian* and the *NOTW* are engaged in this process, there are differences in their portrayals of 'the paedophile'. They construct the same discourses but differ in terms of frequency of use (e.g. the discourse of violence is much more popular with the *NOTW*), stereotyping (e.g. the *NOTW* constructs paedophiles as simply evil *beings* while the *Guardian* portrays them as carrying out evil *acts*) and choices (e.g. the *NOTW* primarily uses the discourse of perversion while the *Guardian* prefers the discourse of pathology). Further, the *NOTW* is more coherent because the *Guardian* allows countering voices which disagree with general discourses or editorial lines. There is also a degree of inflammation and sensationalism in the *NOTW* which is not present in the *Guardian*; this is exemplified in the fabrication of photographs, gigantic headlines and words such as 'perv' or 'paedo'. Nevertheless, there is unity as both newspapers use the same discourses. If we understand the world through discourses, the *Guardian* offers us a slightly different but not radically alternative way of understanding issues around paedophilia.

As for the relationship between the media and the focus groups, there is generally a considerable overlap, as participants often understand paedophilia through the same discourses as the media. This expresses itself forcefully in processes of recognition, which are informed by the discursive figure of 'the paedophile'. However, there is incongruence and discord as some individuals actively reject or ignore aspects of media discourses. Hence the media possess *some* power to shape understanding and practices, such as recognition, through discourses. This power plays out differently for different discourses for a variety of reasons, one factor arguably being the crudity of a discourse. The cruder a discourse, the less likely it is to be accepted, which could explain why the discourse of cunning is more popular than the discourse of perversion. Individual responses to discourses were mediated by political outlook(e.g. liberal participants in group 2 were disinclined to subscribe to discourses of evil or violence) as well as by personal circumstances and subject positions, which encourage individuals to take an interest in and remember discourses, but not necessarily to agree.

The process of categorising of paedophiles occurs alongside the process of individualisation–universalisation, which conceptualises paedophiles as universal individuals. As a result, paedophiles are simultaneously constructed as knowable and unknowable, as an identifiable type of person and potentially anyone. The contradiction at the heart of the two processes repeats itself in the discourses involved in the construction of 'the paedophile'. They construct 'the paedophile' as encompassing binary opposites, such as evil and cunning, normal and abnormal, rational and instinct-driven, human and animal. The dangerousness of the figure of 'the paedophile' is located in these ambiguities and contradictions, rather than simple negativity. The potential of paedophilia as a social problem inciting fear has to be understood through this highly dangerous, universalised discursive figure, as well as through media constructions around numbers and statistics discussed in the next chapter.

4

The paedophile risk: scales, fears and the Internet

The previous chapter has shown that understanding of paedophilia is structured around the figure of 'the paedophile', which designates certain people, activities and spaces as either safe or dangerous, and possesses the potential to incite fear. This chapter deals with the quantitative dimension involved in the construction of paedophilia. It is concerned with the scales of the paedophile risk, how the media and focus group participants assess and construct the size of paedophilia as a problem, and how emotions such as fear and worry may be linked to them. Very little is known about the numbers of active, let alone passive, paedophiles because research into this area is notoriously difficult (Howitt 1995). The focus here is on the way in which media representations of scales and sizes may shape popular risk assessments and concerns. The second half of the chapter focuses on the Internet as a distinct sub-theme of paedophilia controversies, in particular how its virtual nature impacts on risk perceptions and fears.

Media constructions of a social problem

Figures and numbers

Scales are central to the problem of paedophilia, providing information about its size. As scales and sizes revolve around numbers they encourage an individual approach: counting paedophiles. The risk or threat perceived is not so much paedo*philia* as the persons who represent it, paedo*philes*. The figure of the criminal displaces the event of the crime, and the discourses of perversion and pathology construct 'the paedophile' as an 'a priori' criminal (Ashenden 2002). Hence, terms like 'paedophile risk' or 'paedophile threat' become more accurate expressions in these debates than 'paedophilia'.

While paedophiles are constantly constructed as a risk, assessments of the scale of this risk vary. Variations are made possible by a lack of research as well as risk conceptualisations. Risks are invisible and knowledge-dependent in their existence, marked by complex cause–effect relations, and exist in a context of reflexivity relativising knowledge (Beck 1992). As a consequence risks are indeterminate and open to debates over scale, urgency or acceptability. The *NOTW* constructs paedophiles as a large-scale, national threat. It creates the impression that paedophiles are in fact so pervasive as to be ubiquitous through two specific claims. First, the *NOTW* claims that anyone could be a paedophile:

> BE ALERT to **any adult**, not just the named paedophile, who is paying an unusual amount of attention to your children. BEWARE **anyone** who has unsupervised contact with your children.' (T. Taras and P. McMullan, 'What to do if there is a pervert on your doorstep', *NOTW* 23 July 2000, p. 2)

Second, the newspaper suggests that enormous numbers of paedophiles are present around us:

> There are **110,000** child sex offenders in Britain.. **one for every square mile.** ('Named shamed', *NOTW* 23 July 2000, p. 1)

The *NOTW* constantly uses quantifications, numbers and statistics to support its claims:

> There are **4000** men aged 20–25 with paedophile convictions and **6000** aged 26–29. **21,000** are in their 30s and **79,000** over 40. (T. aras and P. McMullan, '10 facts to shock every parent', *NOTW* 23 July 2000, p. 2)

Readers will not be able to remember exact figures, but some numbers might stick and the message is made clear (Fowler 1991).

The already large official numbers are further inflated through constant reminders that they are just the tip of the iceberg, due to low reporting, arrest and conviction figures. As a consequence the 'real' figure is constructed as massively exceeding official figures:

> **Every day,** somewhere in England and Wales, there are **at least TEN sex attacks on children by paedophiles.** And in the **43 days** since Sarah's murder, **more than 460 attacks** have been carried out on helpless young victims. [. . .] In 1997 the report records 2794 convictions of child sex offenders for assaults ranging from rape to gross indecency. [. . .] But these figures do not tell the whole tale. An NSPCC

spokesman told us: 'The number of convicted sex offenders is only the **tip of an ugly iceberg**. Many child attackers are never brought to justice. By our estimates **two-thirds of all children never report their sexual abuse** and suffer in silence.' (J. Stenson and D. McGee, '. . . and today more suffer', *NOTW* 13 August 2000, p. 2)

The *NOTW* does not tend to disaggregate statistics to clarify which proportion of these offences have been committed by strangers (Ashenden 2002), and as 'the paedophile' is a stranger figure this omission encourages an interpretation of statistics as referring to stranger incidents.

In order to make large statistical numbers meaningful the *NOTW* converts abstract, aggregate figures into smaller spatial or temporal units which readers can relate their own lives to (e.g. '110,000 child sex offenders in Britain.. one for every square mile', ' Every day there are at least TEN sex attacks on children by paedophiles'). Further, the *NOTW* brings home the risk in a literal way by constantly emphasising spatial proximity of paedophiles:

Statistics . . . reveal the true depth of **depravity** that exists **so close to home**. It is why we must know who are the paedophiles **among us**. (T. Taras and P. McMullan' '10 facts to shock every parent', *NOTW* 23 July 2000, p. 2)

Each one [child] was killed, or believed killed, by the perverts who, until now, **have hidden in our midst**. (Editorial, 'Vigilance not vigilantes', *NOTW* 30 July 2000, p. 6)

These sensational actions are designed to make people relate risks to their own lives and *feel* the threat, and can be accused of manufacturing fear (Cohen 1972). The *NOTW* constructs paedophiles as a huge, ubiquitous and spatially close threat, and just in case any reader still feels unaffected the paper emphasises the unlimited geographical spread of the risk:

Between five and nine children are abducted and killed every year. The grief and despair touches **every area of the country**. (T. Taras and P. McMullan, '10 facts to shock every parent', *NOTW* 23 July 2000, p. 2)

As a consequence of these constructions, Britain emerges as an unsafe place where children are constantly at risk, and where adults should be constantly alert and suspicious of anyone. These constructions were central to the *NOTW*'s 'name and shame' campaign, which had to be justified as targeting a serious and significant national problem.

The *Guardian* is inconsistent and contradictory in assessing the scale of the paedophile problem. In a first phase, lasting until 1 August 2000, its position was liberal, objective and 'anti-panic'. An indicative editorial condemned the *NOTW*'s campaign as a publicity stunt, which is counterproductive, hysterical and misconceived as most child sexual abuse takes place in families. Paedophiles were not really seen as the problem:

> The tabloid tried desperately to **dress this up as a child protection campaign,** rather than a cheap publicity stunt to increase falling sales. [. . .] A better informed public would provide more protection to children, but yesterday's hysterical outpourings will only have increased public anxieties, rather than reduce them. **The chance of a child being abducted and killed by a stranger are remote: about seven a year compared to the 80 killed by family members. Child sexual abuse has a similar pattern.** (Editorial, 'A tabloid horror story: exposing paedophiles is no protection', *Guardian* 24 July 2000, p. 17)

Here, paedophiles are deemed dangerous but not numerous. The paedophile risk is put into perspective, and seen as adequately dealt with by the authorities. Growing fears of paedophiles are dismissed as irrational. These themes were reiterated in various news items and opinion columns at the time:

> The trouble with all this is that, although it is a hideous prospect, it is utterly **absurd for parents to be worrying about the safety of their children. They are at no greater danger than they ever have been in recent times.** The only reason parents are worrying so much is because the tabloids, followed sheepishly by the broadcast media, have realised that playing on parents' fears sells newspapers. (O. James, 'Playing on parents' fears', *Guardian* 20 July 2000, p. 18)

Newspaper politics are important because the liberal and progressive inclination of the Guardian, as opposed to the conservative populism of the *NOTW,* makes it much more critical of traditional institutions, morality and authority. The *Guardian* is generally less predisposed to see crime as a huge problem indicating the moral decay of contemporary society, and more inclined to focus on child sexual abuse as a problem within the family. Nevertheless, after 1 August 2000 the *Guardian* arguably entered a different, second phase, changing its overall tone and position to recognise that there

is a wider, significant social problem of how to deal with paedophiles. The editorial on 5 August 2000 ('After the vigilantes: there
is no easy response to paedophiles') concluded that 'Either way, a
debate is what is needed now.' Another editorial claimed that the
authorities failed to govern the paedophile risk effectively, resulting
in a major social problem:

> Paedophilia is a **hugely under-reported crime**; victims fear they won't
> be believed or feel too ashamed. Few police sources have a dedicated
> pro-active unit which is the only way to unravel carefully concealed
> paedophile rings. . . . That requires a shift of priorities. (Editorial,
> 'The penalties of neglect: paedophilia went too long unconfronted',
> *Guardian* 25 November 2000, p. 25)

Hence, the position of the *Guardian* in 2000 changed with regard
to the scale of the paedophile problem; assessments shifted from
small to significant.

Inconsistency persists as there is still a range of different opinions
expressed regarding the scale of the threat; some commentators continue portraying paedophiles as a comparatively rare threat, against
the editorial line. Contradictions between editorials and opinion
columns are common in contemporary broadsheets as columnists
are allowed to express their personal opinions, which might not be
in line with that of the editor (Seymour-Ure 1998). However, over
time inconsistency regarding the scale of paedophilia has even come
to mark editorials. For instance, in October 2003 a *Guardian* editorial portrayed paedophiles as a serious threat:

> The move [Microsoft closing down its Internet chatrooms] has been
> welcomed by the NSPCC as a welcome step towards protecting chil-
> dren online. . . . These sentiments will be echoed by millions of people
> in the wake of a **series** of scandals in which paedophiles have used
> internet chat rooms to make contact with children in order to 'groom'
> them for subsequent meetings. . . . [T]here is a dilemma: would
> parents prefer their children to be using areas provided by the likes of
> Microsoft – with at least the possibility of providing technological
> solutions to the problem – or using a swathe of really dodgy chat-
> rooms. . . . It is not an easy call. **A serious debate is urgently needed**.
> (Editorial, 'No room for doubt', *Guardian* 24 October 2003, p. 23)

Paedophiles are constructed as a significant and pressing
problem which needs solving. For example, the *Guardian* generally
welcomes the Microsoft move of closing down its unmoderated

chatrooms because of the threat paedophiles pose to children. Further, terms like 'series' and calls for a 'serious', 'urgent' and 'needed' debates portray paedophiles as a pressing social problem. This stands in contrast to a 2003 editorial rejecting radical measures, such as a national police force or paedophile unit, because of the small scale of the stranger paedophile threat:

> Adding a national paedophile unit, when **only six children are abducted by strangers a year**, does not look productive. Murder inquiries need local knowledge. What is needed is more systematic support. (Editorial, 'Accounting for Huntley', *Guardian* 18 December 2003, p. 27)

Overall the *Guardian*'s position on the scale of the paedophile threat has changed and is still changing, oscillating between assessments of the threat as large-scale and as rare. Generally speaking, the *Guardian* and the *NOTW* are united in creating the paedophile risk by constructing it as significant and disseminating knowledge and awareness on a mass scale, but compared to the *NOTW* the *Guardian* remains quite understated. There are no constant suggestions that paedophiles are so numerous as to be ubiquitous and it lacks inflammatory language, meaning that the *Guardian* does not create the same atmosphere of fear.

The idea of ubiquity is not only actively constructed by the *NOTW* but also rooted in the conceptualisation of paedophiles as a risk. Beck (1992) argues that risks are future-oriented. They are the anticipation of a threat, of bad things that might happen and are expected to happen but have not happened yet. This makes risks unreal and immaterial; their existence is knowledge-dependent. When an issue is conceptualised in terms of risk the focus of debate is future occurrence, which can never be predicted in any definite way. Risks are in this sense indeterminate and incalculable. In the case of paedophilia, the only certainty is that paedophiles are the source of danger and that paedophile crimes will happen. The details of occurrence such as who, where or when are unknown. The flipside of indeterminacy rooted in futurity is that the risk might happen anywhere, any time, to any one person. This is a theoretical possibility, not a practical assessment of scales or likelihood, but these two issues are easily conflated in media coverage. It is difficult for anyone to argue against the large scale of the paedophile problem because as *a risk* it is at least theoretically omnipresent and can be constantly suspected.

Images and scales

While this book focuses on language as a mode of discourse construction, discourses are multi-modal and encompass language, images and practices (Hall 2001). The *NOTW* functions as a case study here to illustrate how images can be involved in the construction of certain discursive understandings of paedophilia, specifically the idea of the ubiquitous scale of the paedophile threat.

The first edition of the *NOTW*'s 'name and shame' campaign on 23 July 2000 contained two pages (pp. 2 and 3) of key revelations. In terms of spatial arrangements the right-hand page shows 49 passport-sized pictures of paedophiles. The left-hand page contains a huge, capitalised headline ('Does a monster live near you?'), the corresponding main article with the names and areas of residence of those pictured, and two smaller articles. Following Kress and Van Leeuwen (1996), in such horizontal page structuring the right-hand side contains the more controversial and salient information, and the *NOTW* draws the reader's attention to the photographs in several ways. First, size is important as covering an entire page with pictures provides visual density. Second, as Jordanova (2000) has pointed out, portraits always command attention. Third, attention is gained through framing. The strongly framed headline on the top left commands immediate attention. The black background of the headline merges into a thick black line which continues down the middle of the two pages, and leads on to frame the paedophile picture collection on the left, bottom and right. This line leads the eye from the headline straight on to the pictures, and ensures that the headline is seen to apply to and provide the interpretative framework for the photographs (i.e. these people are monsters; do you recognise any of them?). However, the middle line also ensures a relative separation, indicating that one side can be read and understood without the other (Kress and Van Leeuwen 1996).

The photographs on the right-hand page are all passport sized, showing faces only. They are not portraits in the fullest sense, as the subjects did not model or pose, but they depict potentially recognisable persons and privilege faces. Photographs are a special kind of portrait. In contrast to paintings and other images they are widely seen as directly and truthfully representing reality, i.e. as showing what people really look like. Photographic portraits are therefore ideal for the *NOTW*'s campaign of making paedophiles visible and identifiable. As portraits they invite viewers to pay particular

4 1st edition of the 'name and shame' campaign, *News of the World*, 23 July 2000

attention to certain people, and as photographs they can claim real likeness (Jordanova 2000), which is crucial to recognition.

The photographs as such 'prove' to the viewer that evil exists, that it does have a face or indeed many faces. Showing photographs of paedophiles makes them and the stories told about them all the more true, due to the cultural importance of the visual image, especially photographs, in establishing the truth (Graddol 1994). The pictures display some common features. Nearly all paedophiles are male (46 out of 49), all are white and most are old, with the remainder being middle aged. However, these aspects are not expressive in themselves and could be interpreted differently in a different context. This is especially true as all pictures are of faces only, i.e. viewers are deprived of bodies or contexts which might contain further interpretive cues. Sontag has captured this problem of the unspecific nature of photographs, and the solutions devised by moral campaigners such as the *NOTW*:

> What the moralists are demanding from a photograph is that it do what no photograph can ever do – speak. The caption is the missing voice, and it is expected to speak for truth. (Sontag 1979: 108–9)

Hence, the *NOTW*'s headline is crucial in attributing meaning to the photographs and providing a reading framework. It informs readers about the evil of those pictured, evil that they cannot detect with their eyes. Once this framework is established, the ordinariness of these pictures can be read as proof for the claim that paedophiles are a ubiquitous threat because it supports the postulate that anyone could be a paedophile.

In terms of composition, it is important that the *NOTW* emphasises both the individual and the collective nature of the paedophile problem. Individuality is stressed through the photographs, which depict individuals rather than groups, are of close-shot nature and possess individual captions. Further, white lines running vertically between photographs separate them. The connectedness of the pictures is emphasised through the common headline, the standardised picture size and the grouping of the pictures in an edited collage. This collage is framed on three sides by a thick black line, and further drawn together by the black rows containing captions running uninterruptedly beneath the photographs (Jordanova 2000; Kress and Van Leeuwen 1996). These strategies simultaneously construct paedophiles as individual risks and as a collective, collaborative threat. The collective aspect ensures that paedophiles are seen as an overall, systematic, widespread threat – rather than an occasional individual deviance – which amplifies the threat potential. Constructing paedophiles as an individual risk ensures that attention is not deflected away from individual responsibility, and that every individual is seen as a big threat by and in himself or herself. The focus on the individual and the collective is linked to processes of categorisation and universalisation. Photographs can function to 'establish and delimit the terrain of the other, to define both the generalised look – the typology – and the contingent instance of deviance and social pathology' (Sekula 1986: 7). In the first edition of the 'name and shame' campaign, paedophiles were visually represented as a category and as individuals, as a certain type of person and a large-scale threat. This reflects and visually reinforces the twin processes of categorisation and universalisation.

While language and images work together to produce discourses around paedophilia, understanding and meaning seem to depend more on language than on images (Fairclough 1989). This pattern is grounded in the particular strengths and limits of linguistic text and images as communicative media. Texts rely on language, a complex system which constructs meanings in very direct, precise and nuanced ways. It is a means to describe the world directly and exactly, and to prescribe certain interpretations while excluding others. It can cope with the most abstract and complex concepts, and can pinpoint or close meaning through its specific nature. The disadvantages of language concern the obvious, and hence con-testable nature of the lexical level. In contrast to language, visual images are less direct, precise and prescriptive, and more open in terms of meaning (Sekula 1982). In the case of paedophilia this makes images dependent on language because newspapers want to communicate some specific, detailed and sometimes abstract dis-courses (e.g. evil, cunning) to their readers for which they need lan-guage. Moreover, many of the available photographs are relatively ordinary and not expressive in themselves, simply showing human beings.

Knowledge around paedophilia is produced linguistically and can be used to interpret pictures of paedophiles. Readers need to know about evil to see evil. However, visual images are very powerful. They have a higher truth value than language, are more convincing and can be interpreted as 'proving' that things and persons really exist. The popular belief is that photographs never lie (Graddol 1994). They can be produced, framed, edited and combined to convey certain meanings, such as the group identity of paedophiles. The fact that meanings are not as closed also means they are not as contestable, especially as most readers are quite untrained and unsuspicious with regards to the meaning constructions of the visual. Images are easily and quickly accessed, and possess immediacy and appeal which attract readers' attention. The ability to show also enables images to make specific persons and objects literally visible and recognisable. Thus images and their capacities are more than simply supporters of linguistically established discourses; they were after all at the heart of the *NOTW's* campaign and its success.

Public perceptions and assessments

All focus group participants see paedophiles as a significant and real threat. However, individual assessments of and responses to scales vary considerably and are discussed. Group 3 is the only group where participants do not debate scales but unanimously judge the paedophile risk as so huge as to be pervasive:

> A. M.: So what kind of threat do you think paedophiles are these days?
> Sarah: Very big threat.
> Everyone: Very, very big.
> Sarah: I think it's.. got more.. now.
> Donna: But that's why I can't let the kids out and play anymore, they're [paedophiles] everywhere.

And they believe the risk to be increasing:

> Sinead: It's increasing though, there's more and more.. of them [paedophiles].
> Sarah: And it's like nobody's doing anything about it.. and all these children are getting abused.
> Beth: That's why there's more of them cause nothing's being done.

These assessments of the paedophile risk as great and growing are shaped by various factors. The media are certainly important. Most people today are aware of paedophiles *as* a risk, and the media as a public forum are central to the dissemination of this knowledge and awareness on a mass scale. This brings risks into existence and makes them real in the sense of having real consequences (Beck 1992). Moreover, the media are extremely preoccupied with paedophilia as a topic and actively construct it as a significant risk. In the above example, the *NOTW*'s opinion that high paedophile figures are partly due to the authorities being complacent is reiterated (e.g. 'That's why there's more of them cause nothing's being done'). The second important factor shaping risk assessments concerns direct experiences, which are structured by social class. Participants in the third group have extensive experiences of paedophiles being moved to and living in their area:

> Donna: But there's one [paedophile] near you, isn't there?
> Dorothy: He, he was there . . . and nobody *knew*.. that he was a paedophile!
> Fiona: Was he re-housed there?
> Donna: Yes, he came from Wythenshaw and they dumped him in Rusholme [area where participants live].. near loads of kids!

There is a sense of anger and powerlessness as these participants feel that paedophiles are being housed in their vicinity because of its poverty:

> Donna: Yeah, they [paedophiles] do it in their areas and then they get dumped here.
> Sarah: Yeah, cause it's poor.. well, classed as a poor area.

At this point the strengths and limits of risk analysis emerge. Beck (1992) maintains that risk distribution is largely equal and only to an extent tied to social class and material inequality. Risks initially tend to accumulate at the bottom of the social hierarchy but as they proliferate and intensify they become increasingly universal. The possibility of buying protection and relative safety disappears. In the case of participants' experiences, class positions and risk positions correlate directly; distribution of and exposure to paedophiles as a risk are structured by social class and economic situations. After paedophiles are released from prison, authorities often have to provide housing, and many released paedophiles are housed on council estates. As a consequence those living on council estates, like the majority of participants in group 3 and generally people from lower socio-economic backgrounds, are often spatially close(r) to paedophiles and feel themselves to be more at risk. They do lack the financial means to purchase security, even if any safety purchased can only ever be relative as no one can buy their way totally away from paedophiles. Hence risk assessments are shaped by direct experiences and the socio-structural positions which impact on the distribution of risk. Risk consciousness is not always a second hand non-experience or beyond experience as Beck suggests. In this context it is not surprising that the third focus group unanimously believes paedophiles to be a large-scale threat; the claims of the media match their real-life experiences.

Challenging media representations

However, when this congruence between media representations and personal experience is not present there is more debate and less uniformity regarding the scale of the paedophile threat. The vast majority of focus group participants subscribe to the media discourse of paedophiles being a large and significant threat, yet some individuals challenge these assessments. These challenges take similar forms in groups 1 and 2. Miles and James (group 1) and Hannah (group 2) see paedophile crime as relatively rare and challenge large-scale assessments through a media critique. They suggest that the media exaggerate the risk by reporting an enormous number of instances of paedophile crime:

> Miles: We hear *every* time there's an instance [of paedophilia] with a child.
> Jack: No we don't.
> Miles: We hear about it in the papers.
> Amy: But I don't reckon we do either.. they probably hide it quite a lot.

> James: They [newspapers] have it **all over the pages**, do you see what I mean?

This critique is vigorously disputed by the majority, yet James and Hannah continue their challenges by dismissing the media's high reporting of paedophile incidents as hype and scaremongering:

> James: I think there's quite a bit of **scaremongering** as well, problems are **exaggerated**, I mean **obviously** you being a parent, like.. I'm not a parent so it's not gonna affect me as much.. emotively.. but, I think, realistically, I don't think, I mean obviously there is a massive threat but it's not.. as much as like.. the papers make out.

> Hannah: The thing is all the **scaremongering** as well, it's so difficult to separate away from.. the *constant* bombardment from the media, constant images, the constant fear that it could happen to your child.

This media critique is not the only challenge. Certain individuals question common assessments of the paedophile threat as large-scale through numerical comparisons. By comparing paedophilia with other prevalent crimes, such as robbery, they attempt to contextualise and relativise the scale of the paedophile problem:

> Miles: I think you've gotta look **in relation to other crimes** as well, I mean, it [paedophilia] is a very, very small minority, Jack.
>
> Jack: But the thing is, we don't know!.. how small it is.
>
> Miles: All's I'm saying is paedophilia, although it's very, very serious, Jack.. against robbery or.. I don't know, maybe murder.. there's probably not as many instances.. so you could say that.. let's forget about robbery because paedophilia is more important.. but on a grand scale of things.
>
> James: It [robbery] affects more people. . . . **in terms of numbers** at least.

By comparing paedophilia to other risks facing children, such as accidents in the home or on the streets, Hannah tries to emphasise the relatively low probability of your own child becoming a victim of paedophile crime:

> Hannah: Anything can happen to your child, it's not just a paedophile, your child could get knocked over, your child could fall down and bang their head, your child could fall down the stairs.. and I actually think those things are far more worrying than having.. worrying about paedophiles, cause **they're so rare** but anyway.
>
> Emily: But I don't think it is so rare.. I mean there's been lots of incidents.. particularly at my daughter's primary school.. people are pulling up.
>
> Vic: Yeah, there's lots of things in the press.

These debates demonstrate the variety of perceptions and assessments of the scale of the paedophile risk. In contrast to the figure of 'the paedophile', which was marked by much uniformity and agreement, the scale of the threat is vigorously argued over due to diversity of opinions. This is possibly grounded in numbers and statistics being more obviously constructions than discursive figures. Individuals are more suspicious of numbers and find it easier to dispute and condemn them as fabrications or exaggerations. The media themselves have popularised concepts based on the notion of 'disproportion', such as moral panics, hype or scaremongering. Numerical claims can be easily fit into these interpretative frameworks as the idea of disproportion is rooted in numerical comparisons. In that sense the media have to some extent facilitated the critique of their own claims.

However, neither media-based challenges nor comparative numerical arguments can change the opinion of the majority of focus group participants, who remain convinced that paedophiles represent a large-scale social problem; and it is this assessment which frames the debate. Those arguing in the examples above that the threat scale is comparatively small often use disclaimers ('I mean obviously there is a massive threat but'; 'paedophilia, although it's very, very serious'), presumably to demonstrate that despite this moderate assessment they still abhor paedophiles. Such disclaimers are made necessary by a culture of total outrage and condemnation regarding paedophiles, a culture which equates displays of horror with morality and large-scale risk assessments with concern for children. This cultural power also shows in debates being limited to the scale of the threat; the reality and seriousness of paedophilia are beyond challenge and dispute. This is why one participant is able effectively to end a group debate on scales by shifting her arguments on to the seriousness and reality of the threat, i.e. that which no one dares to challenge:

> Kerry: I see what you mean but I just think it's [paedophilia], it's.. a threat that is **real**, and.. and for every parent who.. kind of.. maybe gave it just half a thought and then something happens to a child, I can't imagine how they must feel.

Fears

Focus group participants relate to the paedophile threat not only through rational, cognitive assessments of scales but also through emotions. Generally speaking, in all three focus groups there is a sense of parents (23 out of 27 participants) being afraid and worried about paedophiles. This fear is sometimes expressed directly:

> Vic: I must admit if she [daughter] doesn't come home from school, she doesn't come through that door by quarter to four.. I'm on pins and . . . I must admit.. children.. people kidnapping her.. yes, I think that has happened.

> Christine: I think that now cause.. our daughter.. she's only eleven and she's got to go to this new school, and it's miles away so she's got to get two buses.. it takes her more than an hour, and she's only eleven so I went to the school and.. I worry about abductions, but I didn't say that, I only said I was unhappy.. cause she had to travel all this way.. by herself.. cause there's nobody else, but they don't care.

Even parents like Hannah, who assess the paedophile threat as relatively small-scale, are afraid and worried about the safety of their children:

> Hannah: I get really worried if Sarah disappears at Wacky Warehouse
> if I can't see her.. and I climb to the top to make sure there isn't an
> adult with her up there.. so yeah, I would lie to say that I'm not
> worried but rationally.. I, that's an emotional thing, rationally I
> think it's just so much more dangerous to cross the road!.. you know.

This suggests discrepancies between doing and saying, actions and opinions, in the case of some participants. Hannah is aware of these contradictions, while other participants like Ellie claim to be unworried while clearly displaying the behaviour of a worried parent:

> Ellie: It's not even.. I wouldn't say it's [paedophilia] at the forefront of
> my mind.. but every day.. it's a fear that I have.. but I'd be more con-
> cerned if she [daughter] ran off and.. you know, near a road.. but in
> places like parks then.. I might look around and see who's there.

In all examples fear and worry are clearly visible in participants' actions. Hannah makes sure that her daughter is not by herself with another adult in the playground, Ellie scans the park for potential paedophiles and Christine complains to the school about her daughter having to travel by herself. These are actions motivated by genuine worries about the safety of their children because of paedophiles. However, discussions like focus groups are in themselves incitements to fear; carrying out research into paedophilia suggests that it is a significant problem which needs to be worried about. Moreover, the discourse of the good parent (Lawler 2000) encourages the explicit expression of fear as an indicator of care for the safety of your children. This is further reinforced by a cultural attitude which equates assessments of the paedophile risk as large-scale with taking moral responsibility for a serious problem and caring for children. This does not mean that fears are not genuine, but that the expression of fear is encouraged in a number of ways.

In this context discrepancies between what individuals say and do, their opinions and practices, are important. Discrepancies connect to the dichotomy of cognition versus emotion. Some individuals cognitively know and say that the chances of their children being victimised by paedophiles are statistically small, yet on an emotional level they experience concern nevertheless. This suggests that fears are not simply incited by contexts such as culture and research. Some individuals, like Ellie or Hannah, do not *want* to appear too worried. They portray themselves as rational assessors of a statistical risk, and refuse to adapt their cognitive risk assessments to those of the majority. Yet on the level of emotions they are worried, and worries translate into restrictive and protective forms of governance. Hence, as far as the scales of the paedophile risk are concerned, the power of the media may lie especially in their ability to impact on emotions. However, it is important that the attributes and labels which encourage the expression of fear are connected to the level of emotions rather than rationality or cognition. For example, being a good parent is marked by emotional attributes and responses such as care, concern, love and altruism. Indeed, altruism and love are often considered antithetical to (instrumental) rationality. Hence, it is possible to assess the paedophile risk *cognitively* as small in scale and still portray yourself as a good parent; but it is much less possible to be *emotionally* unconcerned about your child's safety in relation to paedophiles and be seen as a good parent. Parents who present themselves as unconcerned are likely to be classed as emotionally detached, which does not fit the discourse of the good parent. The expression of 'rational emotional' responses is more strongly discouraged than the expression of 'rational cognitive' responses, which may explain why rational, cognitive risk assessments fail to match emotions and translate into practices. Fears of paedophiles are genuine but encouraged by a complex interplay of discourses and meanings.

The Internet

In the last few years in particular the Internet has become a distinct and significant sub-theme of paedophilia controversies. In relation to children the Internet is generally understood through a dystopian discourse which focuses on risks rather than opportunities (Young 2001), and this understanding forms part of a trend. Historically, the dystopian discourse has accompanied many media technological inventions, such as radio, television or video (Craig and Petley 2001), and many of those fears have focused on children, for instance in debates around television violence and children. As far as paedophilia is concerned, concerns about the Internet focus on two issues: child pornography and paedophiles contacting children via the Internet. I want to focus on the latter risk because it concerned my research participants more directly, and because much has been written on child pornography and the Internet (e.g. Taylor and Quayle 2003). One of the key issues, in the context of this chapter, is the impact of the virtual nature of the Internet on risk constructions and perceptions of paedophilia.

'Grooming' and identity play

Paedophiles are generally seen to pose a risk to children through 'grooming' behaviour, i.e. a process in which they arguably befriend children to win their trust and ultimately sexually abuse them (Lumby 1997). In the context of the Internet this becomes *the* problem identified and talked about because paedophiles are seen as gaining particular powers. Virtual communication, the argument goes, enables paedophiles to disclose only certain things about themselves and to take on pretend identities, e.g. to pose as a child or pretend to have certain hobbies and interests. In short, cyber-space's virtual reality and anonymity permit unlimited identity play, and manipulative paedophiles exploit this capacity to their advantage. This makes 'grooming' particularly dangerous, and by implication the virtual space becomes more dangerous than 'reality' as it allows for the concealing of 'true' identities (Leaning 2002):

> Danielle Rowland believed Christopher Baxter was the boy of her dreams when they met in an internet chatroom. But the 'hunky, 17-year-old model' she flirted with online turned out to be a **fat, balding pervert** who sexually assaulted the naive 13-year-old. Danielle, now 16, is now determined to warn others about the grooming tactics used by abusers like Baxter, **41**. . . . 'He seemed really **up on all the latest PlayStation games** and knew all the ways to cheat', said Danielle, from Darfield, South Yorkshire. She met Baxter when she started going to chatrooms to talk to other kids about PlayStation games. (N. Cohen, 'Pervert snared me with his web of lies', *NOTW* 16 January 2005, p. 40)

Broadsheets such as the *Guardian* are not as sensational in their language as tabloids; they report on the positive features of the Internet and do not claim that 'grooming' is a common phenomenon. However, understanding of paedophilia as an Internet problem rests in both cases on concepts of 'grooming', anonymity and identity:

> Most chatrooms offer the opportunity for **harmless** if inane conversations. [. . .] With no checks or balances to prohibit access there is little to stop . . . abusers from **posing as kids** to win the confidence of potential targets. [. . .] The abuser will initially **strike up a relationship** by

discussing apparently shared interests such as music, before attempt-
ing to **arrange a meeting** or elicit the child's address or mobile phone
number. (P. Kelso, '**Danger lurking** in the chatrooms', *Guardian* 10
August 2002, p. 4)

Technology offers great fears and fascinations for both papers,
and the Internet is portrayed as inherently risky rather than danger
being the outcome of use in context. This is partly due to understanding being rooted in the discursive figures of the naïve, innocent
child who is easily victimised, and the cunning paedophile who
exploits the possibilities of the Internet. These figures predispose
children as victims and paedophiles as manipulators, and make it
possible for debates around the Internet threat to be simultaneously
based on technological and socio-individual determinism. Media
understanding of children and the Internet is grounded in the view
that technology impacts on children's lives in a direct and necessarily negative way due to its internal logic (technological determinism)
(Valentine et al. 2000). The Internet is inherently risky and the
outcome does not depend on the individual or social-context
factors, such as what is being consumed, where technology is used
or for what purposes. In contrast to this, the understanding of the
Internet in relation to paedophiles is marked by socio-individual
determinism. Here, technology can be used in whatever way and for
whatever purpose; the individual, in this case 'the paedophile', exer-
cises total control.

Socio-individual and technological determinism are both problematic. Any outcome of technology use cannot be seen as inherent
in either the technology or the user but depends on the context, and
any risk potential for individuals varies depending on context
factors (Valentine et al. 2000). Leaning (2002) has criticised popular
views on pretend identities and anonymity by arguing that humans
enter a relationship with technology when using it. As a result any
actions or communications are the product of the interacting agencies of technology and human volition. Those believing that individuals completely manipulate technology, for instance to present
different identities, arguably ignore the interaction between humans
and technology, and have a misguided view of the self:

These claims are primarily built around the idea that online we can
completely control the social 'cues' we give out and therefore the self
we present is purely of our own intention. The self here is a purely

conscious entity, a master of its social situation and able to skilfully use this knowledge in the presentation of what the world will know of it. (Leaning 2002: 21)

The conception of the individual actor which underlies the fear of pretend identities, i.e. individuals as conscious, skilful masters of social situations, fits well with many common characteristics of the discursive figure of 'the paedophile' (e.g. hyper-rational, planning, manipulative or cunning). This close fit is possibly a reason why fear of pretend identities has taken off most prominently in relation to paedophiles.

The media's discursive understanding prompts the question as to why the potentials of the Internet are seen as constantly exploited by paedophiles but never by children. Why are children not seen as posing as somebody they are not? In some sense we could expect the playfulness of pretend identities to appeal *particularly* to children. Presumably, this thought is never entertained as it does not fit the discourse of the child as innocent, passive and incompetent. The following example illustrates the media tendency to make events fit pre-established discourses. All major tabloids occasionally investigate the dangers of the Internet through journalists pretending to be children in chatrooms. The aim is to establish whether and how quickly they would be approached by paedophiles. Journalists invariably report having been approached within minutes, yet ironically paedophiles tend not to pretend to be children, which is how reporters know that they are communicating with paedophiles.

The most useful example comes from the *Sunday Mirror*:

> An **evil** paedophile who **cruises** internet chatrooms to **seduce** young girls has been trapped by the Sunday Mirror. **Within just seven minutes** of going online as an undercover reporter – posing as a 12-year-old girl – Fiona was 'befriended' by sick Paul Wolf. [. . .] Those **few minutes** provide a graphic and terrifying example of the **dangers** faced by **thousands** of children across Britain and lays bare the cynical **tactics** employed by **internet perverts**. Brazenly Wolf boasted of his position as a civil servant, clearly hoping to **impress his young prey**. (J. Weatherup and N. Mahmood, 'Snared: The **evil pervert** preying on the internet', *Sunday Mirror* 11 August 2002, pp. 4–5)

The fact that Paul Wolf did not pretend to be a child is not seen as contradicting the concept of pretend identities, or as giving children power in the form of true knowledge. Instead it is turned into a confirmation of the dangers paedophiles pose by claiming truthfulness as a tactic to impress children. Whatever paedophiles do, their actions are interpreted as consciously and carefully planned tactics, and children's responses are invariably to be taken in by this. If a paedophile pretends to be a child then the child befriends him or her and might meet up. If a paedophile claims to be a working adult then this impresses children and equally entices them to meet up. While anonymity and false information are seen to empower paedophiles and disempower children, correct information does not empower children but equally traps them. For the media it is not important what exactly paedophiles do as the discourse of children as weak and naïve predisposes them as victims anyway. Children possess no agency or power which could lead to different courses of action or outcomes.

The one-sidedness of these views is emphasised by a recent study by Valentine et al. (2001) into children's use of information and communication technologies (ICTs). Based on interviews with children aged 11–16, this study revealed that children are just as aware of stranger danger in cyberspace as in public space, and indeed they know that cyberspace is not very different from 'real life'. The children also argued that they were competent and mature enough to take precautions when talking to strangers, and to avoid putting themselves into dangerous situations. Children want to be and are competent at managing their own lives and they regard their safety as their own concern, indicating that they are not as naïve or incompetent as the discourse of innocence suggests. These real children are not totally vulnerable, weak and passive, or in constant need of protection, but their own voices are rarely heard, let alone taken seriously.

It seems that the media have assigned irreversible roles in the paedophile story: regardless of context children are always innocent and incompetent, while paedophiles are always manipulative, cunning and powerful. As shown in Chapter 2, the media do acknowledge the technological competence of children (which often exceeds that of their parents), and this skill is in fact a feature of the popular discourse on Internet abuse. Technological competence is, however, not equated with social competence or used to question the discourse of innocence; on the contrary, technological competence is seen as making children *particularly* vulnerable by exposing them to material and situations which they are too emotionally and socially immature to handle:

Parents will also be targeted by a £1m advertising campaign to encourage them to learn how the internet and chat rooms work, so they can
educate their children about the dangers of communicating with
strangers online. . . . Chris Atkinson, internet safety expert at the
NSPCC [said] 'Computer technologies are developing faster than our
understanding of them and children are often more clued-up and
comfortable using new technology than their parents. For that very
reason, they can be vulnerable to abuse by unscrupulous individuals.'
(S. Millar, 'Chat room danger prompts new safety code', *Guardian* 6
January 2003, p. 1)

While technological competence may not be easily transferred onto
social competence, simply using the former to reinforce conceptions
of children's vulnerability and the discourse of innocence is a further
indicator that discursive roles have been assigned. Children are
always ultimately understood and reproduced as vulnerable or
innocent, no matter what skills they display.

The two discursive figures of the innocent child and the evil paedophile are the basis of technological and socio-individual determinism, and enable the respective claims that paedophiles are in
total control of technology and children lack any power. Aside from
the problems associated with determinism, the media have to be
criticised for applying two opposite forms of determinism to the
same issue in a way which suits preconceived images. The critique
should also aim beyond determinisms to deconstruct discursive
figures, because deconstructions expose the fact that claims about
the huge threat of paedophiles on the Internet are built on serious
flaws. Children need to be incompetent and innocent, paedophiles
need to be cunning and evil, technology needs to control children
while being controlled by paedophiles – otherwise the simplistic
story of the huge risk could not be told.

Virtuality, reality and risk

Notions of anonymity and identity play are firmly connected to virtuality. Virtuality makes spaces like the Internet appear dangerous
by diminishing certain forms of knowledge or information. In real
spaces details such as the socio-personal characteristics of another
person (e.g. age, gender) are known because they can be seen, but
these forms of knowledge disappear with virtuality due to a lack of
visibility. General knowledge can never really inform us whether
somebody is a paedophile, but there is a tendency to equate

ignorance with danger, and visibility and knowledge with protection. As Chapter 3 has shown, these equations are rooted in the
belief that you would visually recognise a paedophile if you came
across one. As a consequence one would expect virtual spaces like
the Internet to be considered more dangerous than real spaces, and
indeed this is what one focus group participant feels:

> Fiona: That Internet's really.. it's quite bad, I think that's one of the
> most *scariest* things. You can protect, you can tell your children to
> run away from strange men or.. scream if anyone touches them, or
> whatever but the *Internet*.. you just, they just think it's.

While the topics of 'grooming', anonymity and identity play are
extremely popular in all newspapers, however, they did not preoc-
cupy focus groups to the same extent. They only featured significantly
in one group, while the other two groups were not at all interested in
discussing the Internet. This illustrates the limits of the power of the
media to shape understanding and fears through discourses. If we
equate lack of interest with lack of concern, it needs to be explained
why virtual spaces are seen as less dangerous. Focus group debates
reveal that for most participants risks associated with virtual spaces
never become quite real; they always remain associated with the
realm of the hypothetical and ideas rather than acts. Participants conceptualise virtuality through notions of seeing, thinking and fantasis-
ing, and reality through physical acts and doing. Generally, fantasy
and virtuality are seen as harmless, for instance paedophile fantasies
are acceptable if they cannot be acted out in reality:

> Jack: In prison ... they're [paedophiles] talking to each other.. alright,
> about their fantasies and whatnot, that's fine.. because, because
> those **fantasies can't come into reality**.

These virtual fantasies only become problematic when connected to
real acts. For instance, the consumption of child pornography –
which constitutes a 'virtual' satisfaction of paedophilic sexual
desires – is considered dangerous only because of a belief that those
who consume child pornography will ultimately commit real-life
abuse. Thus virtual spaces are harmful, but primarily because they
are linked to real spaces and seen as encouraging real-life child
sexual abuse:

> Kerry: Some teacher guy . . . they [police] took his computer and he
> had all these images of.. children downloaded onto his computer..

and he's been prosecuted, and I thought well.. there's no evidence
to say that he's done anything . . . then I thought well . . . it's sort
of like.. if it's like.. steps two, he's on the first rung. . . . He's started
looking at nasty pictures.. and what's to stop him then trying to
have a go.

Virtual spaces and activities in themselves are not considered dangerous, as the danger remains unreal. Generally speaking, then,
connecting risk assessments and space allows for two opposing perspectives. On the one hand, the Internet can be seen as more dangerous than real spaces because its virtual nature allows for easy
access and 'grooming' through identity play. On the other hand, the
Internet could be seen as less dangerous because its virtual nature
means that any kind of contact or abuse remains virtual, verbal and
not real, physical. Bingham et al. (1999) have pointed out that
cyberspace and the offline world cannot unproblematically be seen
as two distinct worlds. Technology and humans (the social) always
interact; technology gets real in concrete situations and practical
applications. In this interaction both aspects possess agency and
produce the overall outcome. For instance, whether the outcome of
the Internet is dangerous or educational depends on who uses it for
what purpose and in what context – there is no set outcome.
However, in the mind of most focus group participants those two
spaces remain distinct, if connected, and the 'unreality' of the virtual
space overpowers media representations of virtual spaces as very
dangerous.

Conclusions

This chapter has shown that just like the figure of 'the paedophile',
media representations of the great scale of the paedophile risk are
also able to incite worries and concerns, at least among parents in
this study. However, media claims about scales are also much more
disputed than discursive figures, and their impact often showed indirectly through parental protection practices. Discrepancies between
participants' actions and opinions suggest that the power of the
media may work particularly on the level of emotions and in conjunction with the discourse of the good parent.

There are significant differences within the media as the *Guardian*
constructs paedophiles generally as a significant risk but not as a
problem of huge proportions. It also lacks many stylistic features

and claims which the *NOTW* uses to create an atmosphere of ubiquitous risk and fear, such as constant use of statistics or emphases on the spatial proximity of risks. It is impossible to know how these differences impact on participants in this study as they, like most people, have been exposed to various media sources and reports over a number of years. The *NOTW*'s message of paedophiles as a ubiquitous threat resonated on an opinion level only with those whose real-life experiences confirmed it. Others remained sceptical and relatively moderate in their risk assessments.

The Internet and its virtual nature impact on risk constructions, assessments and responses in complex ways. Virtual spaces can be conceptualised as both more and less risky than real spaces, and while the media tend to generate paedophiles on the Internet as a huge threat these constructions largely fail to incite concern in participants. Therefore understanding of and responses to paedophiles on the Internet cannot simply be mapped onto general findings, despite shared features such as the major discursive figures. Paedophilia is constructed as a significant risk through discursive figures and numeric claims, as well as the regulative practices of governments and parents. This will be the subject of the next chapter.

5

Governing paedophilia

This chapter centres on how paedophilia is governed. In paedophilia controversies, paedophiles are understood as *a* risk and children as *at* risk and unable to provide for their own safety. In this context parents and the government and its law enforcement agencies become the major agencies governing paedophilia by acting to avoid, minimise and combat the risk. While Chapter 4 has shown that paedophiles are constructed and understood as a significant threat, this chapter deals with how the government and parents respond to this risk by regulating child sex offenders and children. I will argue that these forms of governance are based on and enabled by the discursive figure of 'the paedophile'. Yet as this figure is also constructed as ungovernable, contradictions emerge and produce a situation where increased governance coincides with continuing fears, as the government finds itself unable to reassure the public through increased legal activity. This analysis will be taken further to argue that paedophilia is an issue exposing a crisis of neo-liberal governance by revealing the limits of neo-liberalism and generating disputes between the government, the media and the wider public over forms and rights of governance.

Neo-liberalism and its contradictions

The media construct paedophilia as a significant social problem which has to be dealt with by the authorities. The ways in which the government and its authorities respond are incongruent with their usual neo-liberal style of governance. Neo-liberalism as a rationality of government mixes a free market approach and minimal state intervention with a basic, reduced welfare state and public services. In terms of penal policy there is evidence that crime prevention, detection and management have been approached in a typical neo-liberal fashion and become individualised, e.g. through burglar and car alarms, private security firms or neighbourhood watch schemes (Garland 1999; O'Malley 1996). This has led Rose (2000) to conceptualise government in advanced liberal societies as state rule 'at a distance' where the state has a low-level steering rather than an interventionist role. Paedophilia represents an issue where penal policy and crime control are not congruent with neo-liberal principles, ideals and aims. The government attempts to deal with paedophilia through more laws and tougher punishments of child sex offenders, meaning more convictions, longer sentences and an extension of state surveillance beyond custodial sentences. This is a punitive, authoritarian and protectionist approach revealing the contradictions and limitations of neo-liberalism. The market and individuals become responsible for the provision and regulation of tasks and services in many areas of social life while the state withdraws, but in some areas of crime control the state contradicts this trend by intervening heavily and strengthening state control.

The punitive trend is longstanding and expressed in increased and tougher legal action. The biggest single legal development since the mid-1990s arguably concerns the introduction of the sex offender register in 1997. It requires all those convicted of and cautioned for a sexual offence since 1997 to notify the police of their details (e.g. addresses and names) and any changes. The duration of registration requirements depends on the severity of the crime; those who have received a custodial sentence of more than 30 months have to register for life. Failure to comply is a legal offence punishable through fines or imprisonment. The sex offender register is not open to public access in the UK, as successive governments have consistently refused this form of self-information and regulation (Thomas 2000).

In terms of probation, the Criminal Justice Act 1991 has made it possible to attach a number of additional requirements to probation orders. Since 1995 the release of sex offenders with life sentences can be made dependent on extra-licence conditions which include:

- not engaging in any work or other organised activity involving a person under a given age;
- not residing in the same household as any child under a given age;

- not seeking to approach or communicate with family members including children without permission of the supervising officer. (Thomas 2000)

Since the Crime and Disorder Act 1998, post-release supervision of sex offenders can also be extended to a maximum of 10 years (Thomas 2000). This punitive trend continues, as evidenced in pilot projects such as the electronic tagging of released sex offenders, and in continuing debates about indefinite reviewable sentences.

In November 2003 the Sexual Offences Act was passed, which has introduced several major legal measures concerning child sexual abuse.

- It has created a new offence of 'grooming', defined as befriending a child for the purpose of sexual abuse, either on the Internet or in 'real' space. Child sexual abuse need not have occurred; a person is guilty if travelling to meet or meeting the child in question. The maximum penalty is 10 years' imprisonment.
- Sexual intercourse or penetrative assault of a child under 13 are automatically classified as rape as children under 13 are classed as unable to give true consent. The penalty is life imprisonment.
- Child sexual abuse involving physical contact with a child (e.g. non-penetrative assault or incitement to sex) carries a maximum sentence of 14 years' imprisonment.
- Child sexual abuse not involving physical contact with a child (e.g. engaging in sexual activity in the presence of a child or causing a child to watch sexual activity) carries a maximum sentence of 10 years' imprisonment.
- The category of incest is replaced by the category of 'sexual activity with a child family member', which includes step and foster relations as well as blood relations. It carries a maximum sentence of 14 years' imprisonment.
- The notification requirements of the sex offender register have been tightened and widened.

These legal and political developments have been marked by coherence. The approach to and management of child sex offenders has become increasingly punitive, as evidenced in the creation of new offences, longer maximum sentences, preventative sentencing and a lengthening of control through post-release regulations. This approach has been characterised as a 'community protection model' (Kemshall and McIvor 2004) which prioritises public protection through punitive measures. Further, Kemshall and McIvor (2004) have identified three developments or approaches in the governance of paedophiles: selective incapacitation (of serious offenders), and preventative sentencing and community risk management (of high-risk offenders after their release or as part of a community sentence). Medical treatment programmes exist, as paedophiles are understood as pathological, but these are supplements to punishment rather than solutions. The ideal of rehabilitation has been replaced by a risk management approach.

Recent forms of governance of paedophilia can also be described as interventionist and authoritarian because the government has attempted to solve a problem through protectionist legislation, keeping power firmly in its hands. This contradicts the neo-liberal philosophy of governing through the actors involved, e.g. via self-regulation and self-surveillance (Garland 1999). The Internet is the only aspect of paedophilia which has to some extent been regulated according to neo-liberal principles. Initially, the government tackled the problem of child protection and the Internet by making the Internet industry and parents responsible for content regulation. A self-regulatory industry body (Internet Watch Foundation) was established, and technical systems blocking reception of classified sites, such as net nanny or PICS, were promoted to consumers (Oswell 1999). In 2003 and 2004 the government also funded major media advertising campaigns against Internet paedophiles which were supported by the official website thinkyouknow.co.uk. While these actions represent direct interventions they do not contravene the neo-liberal philosophy. Adverts and the website were designed to inform children and parents about the danger of paedophiles on the Internet, in particular the risks of 'grooming' and pretend identities, making protective practices and regulation the responsibility of individual citizens. However, anti-neo-liberal attitudes have also been extended to the area of the Internet. The Sexual Offences Act 2003 has introduced the new offence of 'grooming' children for sexual abuse on the Internet, representing a return to interventionist policies as the government attempts to solve the Internet aspect of paedophilia through protectionist legislation.

As a result, the issue of paedophilia and the Internet is governed in both a neo-liberal and an interventionist fashion, which is inconsistent in itself and contradicts the governance of paedophilia generally where the government retains its exclusive right to regulation. This incongruence is rendered most obvious in the rejection of community notification, a classic neo-liberal measure which entails the individual taking on responsibility for the management and provision of their own safety, as well as the regulation of paedophiles. This incongruence cannot be explained through the problems associated with giving ordinary citizens the right and power to surveillance of the 'Other', because the government has taken its neo-liberal philosophy so far as to endorse this principle, for instance in neighbourhood watch schemes (Ahmed 2000).

Contradictions may be elucidated by governments mapping out different social issues as the responsibility of either individuals *or* the state. For instance, as far as child welfare policies are concerned, neo-liberal governments have dropped care as a responsibility of the state (e.g. privatisation of child care), but retained protection as evidenced in extensive protectionist legislation (Parton 1991). But this splitting of responsibilities does not make for a coherent approach to governance. Another way of making sense of neo-liberal governance concerns the *need* to intervene in paedophilia. Crime control attempts to achieve the three goals of efficiency, equity and liberty. These aims are not congruent and their reconciliation involves a trade-off which produces a socially acceptable solution (Legrand and Robinson 1984). Such trade-offs concern all questions and decisions involved in crime control and law enforcement, such as defining crimes and determining the severity of an offence or appropriate punishment. These decisions, as well as the goals of equity and liberty, need to consider ethics, morality and collectivity. As the market only recognises monetary or instrumental rationality it has little to say on these matters, making it unfeasible to govern at a distance in all areas of social life (Carrier 1997).

The crisis of governance is not just rooted in paedophilia controversies exposing the limits of neo-liberalism. Indeed the contradictory nature of policies, marked by state interventionism as well as shifting responsibility onto the individual, is not totally novel. Conservative governments in particular have long displayed a tendency to mix free market economics with a strong, repressive state in cultural and moral affairs. Moreover, Garland (1999) has pointed out that, driven by emotional language and moralising, governmental crime management has recently taken a punitive turn.

Arguably, the real novelty and crisis potential of paedophilia is grounded in the production of an extensive critique of the government, and deep disagreement between the government, the media and the people. A sustained critique focuses on particular legal measures and problematises governance itself, as the government's right to retain exclusive access to governance and knowledge is questioned. At this point a genuine legitimation crisis of neo-liberal governance emerges as discourses which function as state legitimations, such as rights or state authority, have failed (Dean 1999a).

According to Ashenden (2002) measures governing paedophilia reflect two different models of citizenship and two categories of regulative responses. Certain measures, such as indeterminate sentences or the extension of maximum custodial penalties, primarily aim to eliminate danger, i.e. to remove paedophiles from society. Others, such as the extension of post-release supervision or the sex offender register, aim primarily at risk management. However, the two categories of regulative responses are connected. Different inflections can be given to the same measures, for instance public access to the sex offender register as campaigned for by the *NOTW* aims at danger elimination rather than (or as well as) risk management. Reviewable sentences mix both regulative approaches by grading 'danger' through risk assessment, with the aim of eliminating the biggest dangers and managing the remaining risks. Ashenden clearly shows that both official and popular responses mix regulative approaches, hence disputes between the government and the wider public over solutions cannot simply be explained by the former adopting a risk management approach and the latter demanding the elimination of danger.

Different regulative approaches are related to different dimensions of paedophilia as a social problem. Paedophilia is understood as both a technical problem (which can be governed through risk management) and a moral problem (which demands governance to eliminate risk). Phoenix and Oerton (2005) have shown how official discourses have recently degendered the problem of sexual offending and violence in all its forms. By rewriting and erasing the social realities of sexual violence, these discourses present sexual offending as a technical problem demanding technical solutions. Yet I would also argue that even in this context child sexual abuse and paedophilia, as opposed to sexual violence against adults, retain a strong moral dimension which is rooted in the moral status of the child (see Chapter 2). The dissatisfaction and disputes regarding regulative measures can to an extent be illuminated through the multi-dimensional nature of the paedophilia problem which always leaves some demands inadequately addressed.

Indeterminate sentences

Indeterminate sentences, where custodial sentences are infinite and release is tied to the fulfilment of certain requirements, are an expression of the trends of selective incapacitation of 'serious' offenders and preventative sentencing of 'high-risk' offenders in the name of public protection (Kemshall and McIvor 2004). The *NOTW* supports this measure in its most extreme form (as 'real life' sentences without any possibility of release), and launches strong critiques against the government which refuses the introduction of such a blanket law. In its critique the *NOTW* deploys discourses of failure and inadequacy, to construct the government and the legal system as failing to deliver justice and protection due to a mix of incompetence, indifference and inappropriate, left-wing leniency.

In summer 2000, the *NOTW* demanded two changes: the introduction of indeterminate sentences and community notification. Rather contradictorily, the *NOTW* demands more action from official authorities while describing them as totally inadequate and questioning their right to govern. The *NOTW*'s critique, especially the charge of leniency, is closely linked to the figure of 'the paedophile'. The discourses of perversion and pathology in particular construct 'the paedophile' as incurable, unchangeable and an inevitable recidivist. In this context lifelong incarceration, i.e. the elimination of danger through the removal of offenders from society, becomes the logical response:

> Currently, soft parole boards and 'good behaviour' remission mean that a **child sex beast jailed for life can be back on the streets within nine years. Many of those men re-offend.** [. . .] But if a judge DOES sentence a man to life, then that **monster must NEVER be set free.** [. . .] Former Flying Squad Commander JOHN O'CONNOR, who spent 30 years in the Met, said: . . . 'I have come across a number of paedophiles and one thing that is clear is that **they will never change.**' (R. Kellaway and B. Begley, **'Lock them up for life'**, *NOTW* 23 July 2000, pp. 4–5)

In the *NOTW*, claims that the authorities' lenient, inadequate treatment of paedophiles leads to injustice and endangers children through re-offending paedophiles are frequently 'backed up' by case stories:

> 'Black had abducted and sexually assaulted a little girl when he was just a teenager', he [Psychiatrist Wyre] said. 'The attack was so severe that she nearly died. Yet he was simply admonished for that offence. The **authorities** said at the time he'd grow out of it and it would be **wrong to label him**. I firmly believe that if he **had been put away then, Sarah, Caroline and Susan would be alive today**.' (A. Gekoski, 'Their **evil** is **incurable** says crime expert', *NOTW* 23 July 2000, p. 5)

These extracts show how complex the relations between regulative approaches and the technical and moral dimensions of paedophilia are. Demands for indeterminate sentences are clearly demands for the elimination of danger, and as such affiliated to moral conceptions of paedophiles as evil monsters who do not qualify for citizenship (Ashenden 2002). Yet these demands are also justified in technical terms, most notably recidivism rates. The discourses of perversion and pathology connect the two dimensions and make it possible to reconfigure the moral as the technical.

The *NOTW*'s position on indeterminate sentences is partly shaped by the paper's politics and general views on crime. Its populist conservatism means that various governments have been accused of being soft on crime, insufficiently punitive and authoritative. These politics stand in contrast to the liberalism of the *Guardian*, which generally supports a view of crime as a complex problem demanding understanding of the causes of crime to develop effective measures and forms of punishment. As a consequence, the idea of total government failure and misplaced leniency is extremely rare in the *Guardian*. It is only expressed by self-pronounced, populist 'anti-liberal liberals' such as Julie Burchill:

> This government is liberal in all the wrong places. [. . .] If you are . . . a paedophile with an average of 300 offences against children by the time you're finally caught (as the average paedophile does), you can expect to be chucked under the chin and sent along home with an ominous 'And don't do it again!'. [. . .] Why do governments, establishments and judicial systems of every complexion do all they can to let nasty people **get away with things**? . . . But no one ever seems to care about making decent, law-abiding people meaner and nastier, which successive **governments' failure to punish evil adequately** has certainly done. (J. Burchill, 'I cannot see murderers swagger out of the

maze without wanting to shut Peter Mandelson's treacherous hand in
a car door', *Guardian* 12 August 2000, p. 3)

Discursive connections between pathology, recidivism and governance are commonly made in the *Guardian*, yet discussions rarely
produce a discourse of total government failure. Generally there is
a much greater range of voices in the *Guardian* as to solutions
regarding paedophilia. In 2000 the newspaper had no official solution, and the opinions of individual commentators diverged regarding the possibility of a cure or the future risk status of paedophiles.
As a consequence, various solutions were considered and put
forward, indefinite incarceration being *one* of them:

> Many hard-core sex offenders seem to belong to the small category
> of people that society must realise are **too driven to be susceptible to
> rehabilitation** and too dangerous to have in the body of society. [. . .]
> The suggested approach is to transfer child sex offenders who have
> completed their sentences and are still considered high risks to the
> community from prison to a **guarded village** or town where they are
> allowed to lead normal lives aside from the requirement that
> they stay put. (A. Etzioni 'Isolate them: paedophiles should be con-
> fined together in special towns', *Guardian* 19 September 2000,
> p. 19)

Indefinite confinement in special towns adheres to the same logic as
the *NOTW*'s indefinite incarceration: both are rationalised through
the 'pathological', 'inherently recidivist' nature of paedophiles.
With the enlargement of the category of dangerous individuals under
neo-liberalism and concepts of incurability, prison as a solution to
crime has arguably been relegitimised, even for liberal commentators
(Pratt 1999).

The popularity of indeterminate sentences is also evident in all
focus groups, and this measure is rationalised through the familiar
logic of pathology and recidivism:

Group 2
Helen: I think there's obviously **extreme cases** [of paedophiles] where..
  you've just got to lock them up.

Group 3
Sarah: I believe.. people like that [paedophiles].. they should be locked
  up.. they don't stop at one, whenever an opportunity arises.. they're
  gonna have that feeling again.

The popularity of indeterminate sentences is illustrated by support across focus groups, including participants in the second group who conceive of themselves as liberals. In a sense similar differences are played out here between groups as between newspapers: for liberal participants as for liberal papers indeterminate sentences and physical separation are one solution among several. Moreover, for liberal participants indeterminate sentences are not a blanket solution but seen as appropriate for extreme cases, for serial recidivists. While participants are critical of the authorities there is no sustained discourse of failure; the critique is usually specific and paired with praise of the authorities.

The key rationale behind indeterminate sentence is usually claimed to be protection, i.e. the future protection of society through the prevention of further crime. As risk is rooted in futurity (Beck 1992) and paedophiles are understood as a risk, the focus is on future offences. However, indeterminate sentences are not simply rational solutions to a technical problem or risk. Pratt (1999) has pointed out that the wider population has adopted the neo-liberal axiom of seeing protection from risk and offenders as their *right*. Further, the rationales behind these sentences involve elements of retribution and punishment; lifelong incarceration is after all the harshest form of punishment available to the British legal system. This wish for retribution shows clearly in some participants objecting to sentences on the grounds of insufficient punishment:

> Beth: They're [paedophiles] not getting nothing, are they?! They're getting out after seven years and they're just . . . they've been in prison, done their term, and then come back out and just carried on.
> Sinead: Like that guy.. raped a kid.
> Lisa: Seven years isn't enough.
> Donna: Yeah, he's done that so even thirty years, that's not enough.

It is not clear what kind of punishment would be sufficient as wishes for retribution have a tendency to be bottomless, e.g. even 30 years' incarceration is declared inadequate. Again the language of risk makes it possible to configure a moral motivation and approach officially as a technical one, but ultimately this moral perspective will not be satisfied by technical solutions. Delivering protection cannot substitute for delivering punishment.

Community notification

The sex offender register is a community risk management tool designed for surveillance and control of sex offenders who are not incarcerated (Kemshall and McIvor 2004). Disputes ensue over whether the public should have access to this register and hence to the names, photographs and addresses of convicted and cautioned 'paedophiles'; a measure which in the US has become known as community notification. Since 2000 the *NOTW* has demanded such access but successive governments have refused to introduce it. In the *NOTW* demands for community notification are tied to a critique of the government as inadequate in the sense of ignoring the wishes of the people. In such arguments the 'common people' are juxtaposed to the authorities. The people are portrayed as having common sense and real-life experiences. They arguably want practical solutions which are effective and fair, which punish offenders and protect victims. The *NOTW* represents itself as fighting for these people:

> I want to thank our supporters, who are many, and answer our critics, who are few. [. . .] **Honest people feel the system is failing them.** Concerned parents who believe they have no **voice** see the only way forward as **direct action. Now they have a voice. The News of the World. And already they can see the results.** (Editorial, 'NOTW campaign', *NOTW* 13 August 2000, p. 2)

In contrast to this the authorities are represented as overly liberal, left-wing, elitist and intellectual. They talk rather than act, are more concerned about offenders than victims and so detached from real life that they cannot recognise the real problems or simple solutions. Moreover, they are portrayed as arrogantly ignoring public wishes, thinking they know best:

> This **arrogant lot** have ventured from their **cosseted, cloistered and comfortable worlds** just long enough to show their **contempt** for your opinions. They know nothing of the **real world,** and show no concern for real people. (Editorial, 'NOTW campaign', *NOTW* 13 August 2000, p. 2)

This is a moral, conservative-populist, anti-intellectual critique which generates a real sense of 'us versus them', the people versus the authorities. This critique provides the moral legitimation for community notification: it is the right of the people to know, to govern themselves.

While the liberal and more intellectual *Guardian* shuns these populist juxtapositions, the *NOTW*'s critique and demands for community notification prove fruitful with some focus group participants:

Donna: **They** [the authorities] should tell **us** [where paedophiles live].
Dorothy: **We** didn't know at all [that a paedophile was housed next to them].
Sinead: When my mum was in Ireland they had a paedophile living next door . . . and they moved him back into that same area.
Pat: That's what I mean, **they** don't tell anyone.
Fiona: **They** should do.
Sarah: I think **they** should tell **us**.

These participants in group 3 are at the bottom of the socio-economic hierarchy and feel disconnected from the authorities who have housed paedophiles in their area without warning or consent. Personal pronouns such as 'we' and 'they' clearly express an 'us versus them' perspective. Participants support community notification and are captured by the *NOTW*'s critique of the authorities because it confirms their own direct experiences. Like the *NOTW* they consider public access to the sex offender register their right, e.g. 'should' implies a moral obligation of the authorities to share information. The *NOTW* plays on feelings of disconnection in its pretences to champion the causes of 'ordinary people'.

The limits of neo-liberalism
Focus group participants and the *NOTW* employ the discourse of rights to legitimise demands for community notification, and to question the government's right to retain exclusive access to information. Hence, at stake is the very right to the govern paedophilia:

It [community notification] is the key to giving every mother and father in Britain a **right we** do not have: the **right** to protect our children from paedophiles. (S. Arnold et al., 'Parent power can change law', *NOTW* 30 July 2000, pp. 2–3)

The government's refusal to introduce community notification is incongruent with its neo-liberal philosophy. Community notification should appeal to neo-liberals as it entails self-governance. Individual citizens take on responsibility for the management and provision of their own safety through the regulation of paedophiles and their own selves, while the state withdraws from these responsibilities. This is in line with the rhetoric of free choice, individual responsibility and empowerment, and the persistent rejection of community notification by UK governments haunts neo-liberalism as it exposes its limits and contradictions.

According to Frank (2001) the market under neo-liberalism is conceived as democratic in that it has no prejudices; within it any tastes can be articulated and any choice can be exercised. In this sense it is portrayed as working on behalf of the ordinary people who are empowered and liberated to choose as they wish. There is no place for elitism, snobbery or hierarchies. Left-wingers and liberals are despised for their arrogant meddling with the economy and social life, and criticised as anti-democratic. On the basis of these claims any critics of the market can conveniently be condemned for their elitism and contempt for the common man. Thus market populism has led to an inversion of traditional images of the left and right, or rather the anti-market and the pro-market fractions. The pro-market, neo-liberal fraction (including the right wing and the new left) is now understood as championing the causes of the common man, as liberating people by giving them freedom of choice and trusting them to make rational decisions. In contrast to this the anti-market fraction (including the old left and liberals) is seen as elitist and oppressive. It prevents people from exercising choices and decisions because anti-market supporters think they know better and distrust the common people.

Of course, this inversion of associations only works if one embraces the ideology of market populism where regulation means depriving people of choice and opportunity, where deregulation and privatisation mean more choice and trusting the people, where consumer choice equals democracy. But it is a powerful, neo-liberal rhetoric which the *NOTW* uses to argue for community notification. It criticises the government and its law enforcement agencies, which reject the measure, as elitist, arrogant and anti-democratic:

> The **government** have been behaving like an **arrogant, self-satisfied elite caring nothing for the views of the people who elected them.** [. . .] But the home secretary leaves the impression he would **rather protect perverts than protect children.** [. . .] Mr Blair's and Mr Straw's time would be better spent dealing with the **REAL problems of REAL people.** (Editorial, 'Listen to the people before it's too late', *NOTW* 17 September 2000, p. 6)

Hence, neo-liberalism has its limits most powerfully exposed through its own language, and these limits concern not only practical policies but also the philosophical foundations of neo-liberalism.

One reason for governments shifting their usual position in the case of paedophilia is probably the highly emotive nature of the topic, which occasionally results in violence. Neo-liberalism's rational-actor model of human behaviour is one-sided and inadequate. Human conduct is informed not just by rational calculations of maximum gain but also by emotions, values and ideologies, which may be irrational or irrational, violent or peaceful. Simply trusting people to behave peacefully is naïve. The neo-liberal rhetoric of trust turns out to be founded on a reductionist and bourgeois model of human behaviour, as well as being a convenient legitimising tool for reducing state obligations. In this context the neo-liberal premises of free choice and being able to act freely according to your own wishes turn out to be potentially detrimental and difficult to apply outside the economic consumer market. You cannot be free to hunt down paedophiles in the same way that you cannot be free to kill. Free choice and diversity of action have their limits, e.g. paedophilia is widely seen as an illegitimate choice. These biases and discriminations are good and necessary because a democratic, fair, stable and socially coherent society depends on constraints. Individuals have to be constrained in the name of the greater good, for the benefit of the wider society. This is arguably what governments have done by refusing public access to the sex offender register, but by doing this they have undermined their neo-liberal conception of society being no more than a collection of individuals.

Governance and concern

Foucault (1978) has suggested that 'the pervert' is one of four figures through which sexuality is regulated. Discourse analysis has shown that while sexuality and the discourse of perversion are clearly important to the production of 'the paedophile', it is arguably more than just another sexual figure or particular version of Foucault's 'pervert'. Compared to 'the pervert', 'the paedophile' is based on non-sexual as well as sexual characteristics and much more detailed. Extremely specific behaviour patterns, such as job choices or certain leisure activities, are portrayed as typical. As a consequence, the figure of 'the paedophile' allows for easier ways of knowing and regulating sexuality than 'the pervert'. Parental and official governance can be shown to be informed by this figure, which marks out certain persons, spaces and institutions as dangerous and to be avoided.

Foucault (1978) argued that the multiplication of peripheral or 'perverted' sexualities in the nineteenth century was part of a trend towards increased regulation and incitement of sexuality. The figure of 'the paedophile' indicates both an extension and a complication of this trend. While 'the paedophile' is central to and enables governance, it is also understood as ungovernable in the sense of being incurable. The dynamics of these contradictory views arguably result in a paradoxical situation of increased regulation and persisting social concern.

Governance through knowledge

Despite direct access to specific data on individual paedophiles, e.g. through the sex offender register, official governance of paedophilia relies on the discursive figure of 'the paedophile'. This is due to specific data such as names and addresses only being available for those paedophiles who have come into contact with law enforcement bodies by being either officially accused of, cautioned for or convicted of a sexual offence against a child. Governance based on specific information can only aim at this section of offenders, and many writers (e.g. Cobley 2005; La Fontaine 1990) have suggested that this is a relatively small proportion of all offenders. Moreover, governance based on specific information is retrospective and in recent years there has been a growing emphasis on preventative crime management. Several acts and legal measures illustrate this trend and how its implementation relies on the discursive figure of 'the paedophile'.

The Protection of Children Act 1999 prevents child sex offenders from getting jobs with children by means of vetting procedures. People who work or apply for work with children have to undergo a full criminal record check so that convicted child sex offenders can be screened out (Thomas 2000). Since the Criminal Justice and Court Services Act 2002 it is an offence for anyone disqualified from working with children, such as child sex offenders, to apply for or accept any employment involving children (Cobley 2005).

The Sexual Offences Act 2003 has created a 'grooming' law, which makes it a legal offence to befriend a child for the purpose of sexual abuse. To be found guilty of grooming, a person has (a) to have communicated with a child under the age of 16 on two occasions, and (b) to have met or travelled to meet the child with the intention of sexually abusing it (Card 2004). In both legal instances discussed here (i.e. vetting and grooming) the law regulates child sex offenders in a detailed way, legally prohibiting particular forms of behaviour such as working with children or 'befriending' children with the intention of abuse. The discursive figure of 'the paedophile' clearly informs these laws as it maps out these behaviours as typical of paedophiles and therefore dangerous. It produces the knowledge on which governance can be based, in terms of both the aims of a law (e.g. to prevent or deter certain people from engaging in certain practices) and legal conditions or definitions (e.g. communicating with a child with the intention of sexual abuse constitutes a legal offence).

In addition to the new grooming law, the Sexual Offences Act 2003 has introduced a number of preventative orders to deal with paedophiles, most notably sexual offences prevention orders (SOPOs) and risk of sexual harm orders (RSHOs) (Card 2004). SOPOs and RSHOs both prohibit the person subject to them from doing anything described in the orders. They differ in the sense that SOPOs can be issued to convicted sexual or violent offenders, while RSHOs can be issued without a conviction and exclusively aim at those who are identified as a sexual risk to children under 16. Like the grooming law, RSHOs aim to identify criminal intentions and thereby prevent crimes from occurring. 'Proof' of criminal intentions is constituted by the subject having engaged in sexually explicit conduct with a child on at least two occasions. Sexually explicit conduct includes (a) sexual activity with a child, (b) inciting a child to watch a person engage in sexual activity in real life or on film (pornography), (c) giving a child anything that relates to sexual activity (e.g. a condom, a sex toy), or (d) involving a child in communication with sexual content.

These conditions and 'proofs' are informed by the figure of 'the paedophile'; 'familiarising' children with sexuality, by means of any of the above actions, is seen as part of the grooming process. Moreover, legislations such as grooming laws or RSHOs define paedophiles as a distinct category of persons which needs exclusive and tailored legal measures, and these measures are necessarily shaped by images of what 'the paedophile' is like.

Generally speaking, legal activity regarding paedophilia has proliferated since the 1990s (Thomas 2000), and the discursive figure
of 'the paedophile' has arguably facilitated increased regulation via
the production of knowledge. The intricate regulations inscribed in
vetting laws, grooming laws or RSHOs are based on and enabled by
the discursive figure of 'the paedophile' which defines certain behaviour and thought patterns, which are not directly 'sexual', as typical
of people with a particular sexuality.

Parental governance

Official and parental governance of paedophilia differ in their targets:
while the former is directed at child sex offenders, the latter focuses
on children. Parental governance of children parallels official governance of paedophiles as both forms are enabled by knowledge of the
discursive figure of 'the paedophile'. However, 'the paedophile' is not
the only important discursive figure involved; the paedophile story
revolves around the three key figures of 'the paedophile', the innocent
child and the good parent (Lawler 2000). These figures are linked in
their constructions and meanings, e.g. the innocence of children
creates a need for adult protection, and connections reveal themselves
in parental governance, which is shaped by all three figures.

The figure of 'the paedophile' focuses parental worries and governance practices onto certain professions and places, such as parks,
ways to school or outdoor play areas:

Sarah: And I've got three little children! And it's like.. I . . . won't even
let them out in the **park**.

Sinead: Even schools though, you get them [paedophiles] there! And
our children can't even walk to **school** anymore.

Beth: I mean to *our* kids *now*, right, if my kids said 'Can we go to the
park?', I'd say 'No!'
Donna: I don't think so.

Beth: But it's like all the free land, you know like a lot of parents say
'Why don't they put a **play area** for kids?' . . . but what's the
point?!.. Do you know what I mean, what's the point cause you
can't let them go anyway, can you.

The detailed nature of the figure of 'the paedophile' allows parents to govern their children's behaviour and movements in very specific ways, e.g. through restricting access to certain spaces or supervising children in certain situations. These particular spaces and situations have been defined as dangerous by the likely presence of 'the paedophile'.

The clearest example of 'the paedophile' structuring governance in specific ways concerns two parents, Celia and Ellie, worrying about childcare arrangements. They are in need of full-time professional child care but making decisions is difficult because of the idea that paedophiles infiltrate professions involving children, such as child care:

> Celia: There was one other stereotype of a paedophile which does bother me and that's **childminders**, I do have a thing about childminders ehm.. we do use . . . a childminder cause we live a fair distance away . . . we put her [daughter] in with a childminder and *that* was a tremendous.. ehm, problem for me to, to find an appropriate person because.. that worries me that.

This worry and belief lead the two parents to regulate their children's lives in slightly different ways. Celia chooses a particular childminder deemed appropriate, and Ellie chooses a nursery instead of a childminder:

> Ellie: I did have the choice of having.. somebody coming to the house and look after her [daughter] and I refused.. because . . . I wanted her with *other* children.. and *other* adults so that, because then it allowed these *other* childminders to police.. the other childminders so.. they all kind of police each other then.

Because 'the paedophile' is such a detailed figure, governance can be as specific as avoiding certain spaces, institutions or people/professionals. However, reflecting the contradictory processes of categorisation and individualisation–universalisation, specific parental regulation is mixed with suspicions that paedophiles are 'universal' individuals, i.e. that anyone could be a paedophile, and that paedophiles could be everywhere. This process of universalisation expands the category of dangerous places and people. For instance, two parents consider not letting their children sleep over at their friends' houses:

> Pilar: I would be more concerned to have my daughter go and.. stay overnight with a friend and.. their parents.. I probably wouldn't do it.
> Ellie: Yeah, that's just strange, isn't it, because.. I know when I was.. younger.. ehm.. we could always go and stay at friends' houses. . . .
> But.. as a parent now I don't know how I feel.

The figure of 'the paedophile' is a stranger figure and participants tend to locate danger in totally unknown people, but some individuals include their children's friends' parents in this category. This could be due to a variety of factors, such as a strong belief in the universality of paedophiles, narrow definitions of what it means to know someone, and/or a lack of familiarity with their children's friends' parents. Spatially, the expansion of danger through the process of universalisation results in some parents not letting their children go *anywhere* unaccompanied. Paedophilia is perceived as a ubiquitous, universal risk which makes *all* spaces dangerous:

> Donna: But that's why I can't let the kids out and play anymore, they're [paedophiles] **everywhere**.

Risk perceptions and fears encourage parental regimes of governance which are restrictive and regulate children's lives, i.e. their movements, time, sexuality and activities. All parental regimes of governance reconstitute the very ideas and figures which fuel them by confirming children as helpless, asexual innocents and paedophiles as a serious risk. These regimes are shaped by the dynamics of the processes of categorisation and individualisation–universalisation. The figure of 'the paedophile' focuses parental governance by marking out certain categories of space and people as dangerous. The process of individualisation–universalisation can increase governance by extending these categories, yet remains limited by the process of categorisation.

Parental governance is not only shaped by the figure of 'the paedophile' but also by the figure of the good parent (Lawler 2000). The two are related because 'the paedophile' as a dangerous stranger is constructed and produced in opposition to the protective, safe parent:

> **Parents:** Ensure that young children do not chat in unmoderated chatrooms. [. . .] Never allow a child to have an unsupervised face-to-face meeting with anyone they meet online. (H. Carter, 'Switching off . . . chatrooms proving too hot for children to handle', *Guardian* 24 September 2003, p. 3)

This is not only the case in the media. Parents construct themselves as good through regimes of governance over their children, regimes which are seen as protecting children from the paedophile risk. The above examples of parental governance have illustrated this well.

The discourse of the good parent requires parents to meet the needs and demands of their children, and in paedophilia controversies safety becomes the key need which parents are responsible for providing, primarily through risk avoidance. Parental governance is clearly a way to represent and produce yourself as a good parent by engaging in risk-avoiding regulative practices.

By implication, these practices construct other parents who do not engage in them as bad, risk-inviting parents (Adkins 2001). Occasionally such parents are directly called irresponsible and bad:

> Tanya: I'm a bit worried about parents that leave their kids on the Internet all the time, and there's paedophiles on it.
> Claire: Yeah, why are they allowed on it and **then they don't want to be blamed** if anything happens.

The discourse of the good parent and the concept of risk are tied to blame. Parents can be blamed for a risk happening to their child because they are considered responsible. Blame, like risk, is a double-edged sword. It is a reflexive tool which can be used to internalise responsibility and to criticise others, to construct yourself as safe and others as a risk. If risk produces reflexivity, reflexivity also produces risk (Adkins 2001). Parents themselves are therefore implicated in the creation of cultural pressures to regulate children and provide safety, as well as the culture of blame. In this context it would be reasonable to expect parental governance to take the form of total restrictions and constant supervision, yet most of it does not. Rather, there is diversity in amounts and forms of parental regulation, and most regulation constitutes a mix of prohibitions, restrictions and freedoms. One participant who sometimes leaves her children unsupervised justifies her practices through notions of freedom and responsibility:

> Kerry: I think a child should be, I mean even in this day and age, should be allowed some kind of.. **his own freedom, his own little world.**

Constant supervision is considered undesirable as well as impractical because of a belief that children should experience some freedom. Thus the rejection of constant supervision is rooted in the discourse of the good mother who not only regulates but allows freedom for the child to develop an autonomous self (Lawler 2000). The dynamics between opposing discursive demands for protection

and freedom may help explain why worry and fear about paedophiles translate into a variety of forms of parenting and restriction, rather than simply constant supervision by all parents.
Variations in risk assessments are probably another factor.

The third discourse and figure shaping parental governance is the
innocent child. Innocence generates a need for protection, a duty
which the altruistic, good parent takes on. Children are seen as at
risk from paedophiles because (a) paedophiles are dangerous and
(b) children are vulnerable 'by nature'. The discourse of innocence
puts children generally at risk by constructing them as incompetent,
naïve and vulnerable. Hence trust in the opposite qualities, such as
competence and being street-smart, should result in less fear, more
moderate risk assessments and less parental regulation. And this is
the case in some respects. For example, parents who trust their children to be competent and sensible allow unsupervised access to the
Internet:

> A. M.: How do you or would you let your children use the Internet?
> Vic: Well, Emma does, she uses the Internet.. by herself.
> Emily: Lynn does, but she is sixteen.. so I trust her to..
> Vic: Yeah, our Emma's twelve but I **trust Emma not to be bloody
> stupid**.

In these cases trust works as a strategy for coping with risk (Giddens
1991). But this trust is difficult to develop and maintain in the
context of a strong discourse of the innocent child, which produces
the widespread engagement of parents in various restrictive and
protective practices. These practices undermine trust in the competence of children by reproducing children as needing protection and
paedophiles as a significant risk. Moreover, they construct parents
who engage in relatively little governance as bad and risk-inviting,
thereby reinforcing cultural pressures to restrict rather than trust.

Risk assessment and the ungovernable 'paedophile'

While the figure of 'the paedophile' enables regulation, it also
renders it difficult and ineffective. The reasons for 'the paedophile'
disabling governance can be identified as (a) risk conceptualisations,
and (b) the nature of 'the paedophile' as a dangerous pervert.

The difficulties of governing 'the paedophile' can be illustrated
well through the popular solution of risk assessment. This method

aims to determine the risk an individual poses by calculating not only the likelihood of offending but also its imminence, consequences and frequency (Grubin 2004). Risk assessment is central to the risk management approach, but as a feature of all major strategies of governance regarding paedophilia it has become connected with a mix of risk management and the elimination of danger (Ashenden 2002). Selective incapacitation aims to physically remove those who have committed 'serious' crimes and are assessed as most dangerous from society, while preventative sentencing is designed to do the same for those who are assessed as very dangerous despite having so far only committed 'moderate' offences. Community risk management aims to control offenders in the community (e.g. through the sex offender register) who have been assessed as a risk which needs monitoring but is not or no longer 'high' enough to warrant custody (Kemshall and McIvor 2004).

The presence of risk assessment in so many legal measures means that it can be taken up and supported in very different ways. For example, the *NOTW* advocates risk assessment in the form of a once-and-for-all procedure undertaken at the time of sentencing. Those deemed a high risk should be given indeterminate, 'real life' sentences:

> Sex offenders should be **subject to a risk-assessment** process at the time of their sentence by the court and indeterminate sentences be imposed in appropriate cases. Where an offender is assessed as suffering from severe personality disorder, and as a consequence poses a significant threat to children, he or she should be detained in secure accommodation. ('Sarah's Law', *NOTW* 6 August 2000, p. 6)

In the 'name and shame' campaign the *NOTW* generated the impression that indeterminate, 'real life' sentences should be given to all paedophiles, in which case risk assessments would be unnecessary. These issues are never clearly mapped out in the *NOTW* as it is concerned with populist solutions, not the intricate details of their feasibility. But it does confirm Ashenden's (2002) point that popular responses to paedophilia are premised on both the elimination of danger *and* the management of risk (even though the *NOTW* focuses on the former).

For both the *NOTW* and the *Guardian* risk is central to a solution to paedophilia, but their solutions and the role of risk assessment within them vary. In 2000 the *Guardian* did not officially support any particular solution, but since late 2001, following the conviction of Sarah Payne's killer Roy Whiting, the newspaper has advocated reviewable sentences where release depends on risk assessment:

> There is a better way to protect families. Roy Whiting, who was sentenced to life yesterday for Sarah's murder, already had a previous conviction of abducting and indecently assaulting a young girl. Prison administrators were concerned by his lack of remorse and refusal to take part in rehabilitation programmes. If there had been a '**reviewable sentence' for serious sex offenders, he would not have been released for his first offence.** (Editorial, 'Sarah Payne's legacy: **no automatic release for sex offenders**', *Guardian* 13 December 2001, p. 23)

The *Guardian* wants sentences which are indeterminate but constantly reviewed on the basis of ongoing assessments of a prisoner's risk status. Thus sentences for paedophiles are possibly but not necessarily eternal as individuals can be released following classification as 'low risk'. This is very much a liberal, softer version of the *NOTW*'s 'real life' sentences. Both solutions are clearly punitive, though, potentially allowing for the lifelong incarceration of offenders based on assessments of the risk of future offending.

The centrality of risk and risk assessment to the governance of paedophiles is not surprising. First, these concepts have become central to penal policy and law enforcement in recent years, especially as strategies for dealing with sex offenders (e.g. Cowburn and Dominelli 2001; Quayle and Taylor 2002). The aim is to determine the risk they will pose in the future through a number of psychological and medical tests. Second, the focus on future risks may be grounded in paedophiles being widely seen as difficult to cure and prone to recidivism. Indeed, risk assessment and prevention are such central issues that they have become the subject of entire documentaries (e.g. *The Protectors*, BBC1, May 2004) and discussions (e.g. Radio Five Live, 9 May 2004). However, there are several problems with the risk assessment approach. Cowburn and Dominelli (2001) and Quayle and Taylor (2002) point to the variety of risk assessment tests, none of which is comprehensive, foolproof or uncontested within science. Yet they claim that for the public the involvement of science and the support of the media for risk assessment raise great expectations in terms of provision of security. Moreover, while risk assessments are ethically difficult, involving decisions about possible incarceration on the basis of future behaviour, they are also ineffective as an overall security strategy because of an exclusive focus on convicted offenders.

Radicalisation of doubt and the dangerous pervert

In contrast to these claims, continuing concern with paedophiles indicates that risk assessment does *not* function to reassure the public or the media fully. I want to argue that these inabilities to reassure the public and govern 'the paedophile' are rooted in two factors: the paedophile as a dangerous pervert and risk conceptions (or the radicalisation of doubt in late modernity). A questioning atti-tude on the part of the public doubts scientific methods and claims to absolute knowledge. This can be illustrated through a radio dis-cussion (Radio Five Live, 9 May 2004) between a radio host and Donald Finnlater, former director of Wolvercote Clinic, which used to offer sex offender treatment programmes:

> Radio Host: Do you say that if your particular clinic had stayed open and was still able to operate now that you could give.. a **cast iron guarantee** that those who've been through what you did there.. would emerge.. and would therefore not pose a threat?
> D. F.: No, well..
> Radio Host: Well, that's the problem, isn't it, there's **no cast iron guarantees**.

Continuing popular worry and concern, and the inability of authorities and science to assuage them, can be partly explained through the radicalisation of doubt in late modernity (Beck 1992). This is encouraged by the awareness that no knowledge is absolute or certain, not even scientific knowledge, and that there are unfore-seen events and unintended consequences. Expert systems and methods are doubted and questioned. In the above example a radio host questions the wisdom of 'psy' sciences by emphasising the inability of this science to predict the outcome of its treatments with *certainty*. 'Guarantee' is the key word here which sums up the hopes and disappointments of the general public. Risk management, whether in the form of risk assessment or rehabilitation, always retains some element of risk or uncertainty in a way that measures eliminating danger, such as indefinite incarceration, do not. Hence, risk management measures work through scientific reassurances restoring some certainty, but these reassurances lose their force in conditions of the radicalisation of doubt. However, while this is true for all crimes, paedophilia is a social problem where this is publicly raised as a problem. In this sense the interview indicates that continuing worry is specifically rooted in the figure of 'the paedophile'; it is grounded in the incongruence between seeing 'the paedophile' as a special type of criminal (a 'pervert') demanding special solutions yet addressing the problem through the common practice of risk assessment.

Several writers (Foucault 1988; Seltzer 1998) have noted that the nineteenth century was marked by a shifting approach to both crime and sexuality. In both cases understanding and focus shifted from the act to the person, from the character of actions to the identity of the actor. A kind of act became a type of person, and in terms of crime these shifts facilitated the concept of the dangerous individual. Seltzer (1998) points out that the rise of the concept of the dangerous individual has generated a new thinking about individuals in terms of the risks they pose, as well as a new solution to crime through risk calculations. The idea of the dangerous individual being assessable in terms of risks makes crimes calculable; they are drawn into the laws of large numbers and away from old associations of sheer contingency.

This approach to crime has been displayed in paedophilia controversies. Paedophilia and child sexual abuse are understood through 'the paedophile' and paedophiles are seen as a risk to be managed through risk assessment. The focus is on future risks as well as on past offences, and the deaths of children are seen as incidents that could have been prevented. However, the idea that you can manage paedophiles through risk assessments is only believed to a certain degree. The future-oriented nature of risk and its knowledge-dependence mean that risks are often largely indeterminate, for example the details of the paedophile risk (when, where, how, who) are unknown. Indeterminacy produces unpredictability and does not encourage faith in risk assessment.

In the case of paedophilia these doubts are further fostered through the discourses of perversion and pathology. These construct paedophiles as incurable and render risk assessments meaningless as the outcome is clear: paedophiles will *always* be a risk. Sometimes they are even conceived as becoming *more* dangerous throughout their lifetimes, meaning that paedophiles are an eternal risk which may become more serious. As a figure at the intersection of crime and sexuality, 'the paedophile' inextricably links danger and perversion. This connection moves 'the paedophile' beyond the category of the merely dangerous individual and turns it into a dangerous 'pervert'. Consequently, the solutions associated with the dangerous individual are insufficient; the dangerous 'pervert' cannot be defeated through the usual means. Methods such as risk assessment become ineffective and paedophiles are rendered ungovernable (Pratt 1999). 'The paedophile' exposes the limits of risk assessment as a governmental penal strategy and solution. More generally, it renders any measure premised on risk management ineffective and constructs the elimination of danger as the only sensible, workable and *certain* approach to regulation.

Authority reassurance and actions fail in such a context, producing a situation where increased legal activity is accompanied by continuingly significant levels of concern. Paedophilia is understood through a figure which is simultaneously ungovernable and relatively easy to govern, a contradiction which has already expressed itself in claims that paedophiles are both recognisable (a category) and beyond recognition (any individual). This explains why increased governance meets continuing concern: the figure of 'the paedophile' renders ineffective the very regulations it enables. It encourages and demands regulation, yet makes it pointless.

If risk assessment techniques are rendered ineffective, trust could be the alternative strategy for dealing with risk. But doubts about the efficiency of risk assessment and the conditions of radical doubt undermine trust too strongly. For Giddens (1990) trust is a strategy for dealing with risk which minimises dangers and fears by dealing with them psychologically. Trust entails a leap of faith but is also based on assessments of risk and security; it balances ignorance and acceptable risk. However, the conditions which make trust necessary, i.e. ignorance grounded in a lack of knowledge and unpredictability, also discourage it. In the case of paedophilia, the figure of 'the paedophile' disables risk assessments and thereby produces complete uncertainty and unpredictability. As a consequence trust becomes impossible and is not available as a strategy for dealing with risk. And if the figure of 'the paedophile' makes trust impossible, so does the figure of the innocent child. Trust is never complete certainty but involves an element of risk which is deemed small and acceptable – yet children are such a moral issue that any risk in relation to them is by definition unacceptable. In these contexts it appears peculiar for the *Guardian* and the *NOTW* even to advocate risk assessment. This peculiarity is possibly rooted in the same condition as the *NOTW* pairing a relentless critique of the authorities with demands for more official action: both aspects might represent instances of radical unthinkability, an incapacity to think beyond existing structures and solutions.

Governing 'the paedophile': the end of liberalism

Bell (2002) has suggested that there is a liberal discourse, as opposed to the populist one, which constructs 'the paedophile' as an offender with human rights who should be given the opportunity of rehabilitation. In contrast to this, Collier (2001) has argued that any such liberal discourse has been overwhelmed by a popular discourse which has become authoritative as it:

> functioned to supersede, and make claims to Truth more powerfully than those discourses which were simultaneously seeking, in contrast, to (re)position the paedophile as within society, as part *of* the social.
> (Collier 2001: 236; original emphasis)

This development seems to have intensified in the years since Collier's writing for it is now difficult even to find liberal or alternative discourses asserted in the public sphere. Hence Bell's claims have to be doubted, especially in the light of the *Guardian*'s support for reviewable sentences, i.e. for sentences which are indeterminate and tie release to risk assessment.

Risk assessment in itself is neither inherently liberal nor populist; as an actuarial technique it can be attached to any political philosophy (O'Malley 1996). But in terms of crime control and penal policy, the liberal approach is associated with the aims of rehabilitation rather than punishment, reintegration of ex-offenders rather than labelling and exclusion, and a concern with the preservation of civil liberties and human rights for offenders (Valier 2002). Reviewable sentences are not really congruent with any of these principles. They are indefinite and make release from custody dependent on scientific risk assessments of future behaviour and dangerousness. As such, reviewable sentences are punitive, infringe the human right to definite sentences, and are ethically questionable as individuals are detained on the basis of acts being possibly committed in the future. The *Guardian* not only supports reviewable sentences but welcomed the government bill of 2002, subsequently passed as the Sexual Offences Act 2003, as 'a good package' (Editorial, 'Straight on sex', 20 November 2002). This bill included raising maximum sentences for many sex crimes and creating new sexual offences. If even a self-professed liberal newspaper consistently supports such a variety of punitive measures, and sometimes lacks concern for the rights of offenders, it is difficult to identify or envisage the bearers of the liberal discourse on paedophilia. This doubt is further strengthened by a parallel lack of belief in rehabilitation in focus groups. Only 1 out of 27 participants advocated it as a solution despite the inclusion of several university-affiliated, self-declared liberals.

Of course one of the features which distinguishes the *Guardian* from the *NOTW* is its greater range of voices (Seymour-Ure 1998). Thus within the *Guardian* there a variety of opinions on solutions, ranging from spatial separation via reviewable sentences (editorial opinion) to rehabilitation:

> If community supervision is to be fully effective, more **treatment programmes** for sex offenders are needed. Treatment programmes aim to counter sex offenders' distorted beliefs . . . and help them to **control** their **deviant behaviour** and avoid relapse. (R. Garside, 'Paedophile watch: **counselling does help curb recidivism** among sex offenders. And **imperfect** though the law is, it's better than baying mobs', *Guardian* 25 July 2000, P. 19)

The *Guardian* is certainly less populist and more liberal than the *NOTW*. Some writers support rehabilitation and there is a strong and widespread opposition to community notification on the grounds that it is ineffective, incites violence and infringes human rights. But this liberalism is neither continuous nor sufficiently extensive to amount to a real alternative discourse and way of understanding. Writers advocating rehabilitation are far and few between, and they are often not *Guardian* columnists (e.g. Richard Garside is a NACRO official). Articles entertaining the possibility of rehabilitation are often qualified, emphasise possibility rather than certainty, and/or rely on specific cases rather than claim rehabilitation as a blanket solution. Rehabilitation programmes are often viewed positively by the *Guardian* but not as a solution in themselves; they are fitted into a framework of providing protection through incarceration. The liberal ideal becomes a good method but not a solution and the punitive, non-liberal trend continues. The lack of a truly alternative, liberal discourse on paedophilia is well summed up by the *Guardian*'s official support for reviewable sentences: more liberal, moderate and flexible than the *NOTW*'s 'real life' sentences, but by no means a really different approach.

Kemshall and McIvor's (2004) analysis of the governance of sex offenders has pointed to risk management being prioritised over rehabilitation, the aim being to control and reduce potential harm (caused to victims) rather than to change the offender. While this supports the hypothesis of the end of liberalism – if rehabilitation is seen as a key feature of the liberalism – the question remains why there is such widespread reluctance and uncertainty regarding rehabilitation. One of the answers lies in the nature of 'the paedophile', especially its pathology and perversion, which renders 'the paedophile' unresponsive to rehabilitation and rehabilitation an ineffective 'solution'. The discourses of pathology and perversion construct paedophiles as sexual deviants, as a category of offenders especially prone to recidivism and very difficult to change. Paedophiles are therefore an eternal risk, which can at best be managed but never fully extinguished.

In this discursive context it is difficult to believe in and support rehabilitation confidently as a solution. However, by being unchangeable, the figure of 'the paedophile' not only undermines the effectiveness of rehabilitation, it also disables risk management and indeed any form of governance which does not physically remove or contain offenders permanently. As 'the paedophile' is unchangeable the elimination of danger becomes the only workable premise:

> Certain people will never be converted into something else than they are. They are, so to speak, beyond repair. One cannot rid *them* of their faults; one can only get rid of *them* themselves, complete with their inborn and eternal oddities and evils. (Bauman 1997: 19; original emphases)

Even if Bauman describes this logic of dealing with the 'Other' as eradicated with modernity, it certainly resurfaces in the populist discourse on paedophiles. While there are some liberal ideas on paedophiles, there is no liberal discourse which fundamentally challenges the populist discourse or offers alternative ways of understanding paedophilia. The lack of truly alternative solutions in the *Guardian* is grounded in a lack of a truly different understanding.

Conclusions

By responding to constructions of paedophilia as a major social problem through interventionist, protectionist governance, the government and its law enforcement agencies, as well as parents, reconstitute paedophiles as a significant threat. Yet government measures fail to reassure the public and result in a crisis of governance. Paedophilia exposes neo-liberal governance as contradictory, arbitrary and flawed in its premises. Moreover, it fuels extensive arguments between the government, the media and the wider public over the adequate governance of paedophiles. This is most acute in the case of disputes about public access to the sex offender register, which involve struggles over the very right to governance.

Increased governance, on the part of both parents and the government and law, is based on and enabled by the discursive figure of 'the paedophile', its detailed nature allowing for very specific regulations. However, this figure is simultaneously constructed and understood as ungovernable, as an eternal risk impossible to control. Being both governable and ungovernable, 'the paedophile' demands regulations yet renders them ineffective. This generates the paradoxical contemporary situation where increased regulation has little impact on concerns. It seems that we cannot govern our way out of fear.

6

Conclusions

Explaining outrage and concern

Moral panic theory accuses the media of being engaged in a process of manufacturing fear (Cohen 1972). The easiest way of doing this is through numbers and statistics claiming that a particular issue is a large-scale problem, and both the *NOTW* and the *Guardian* represent paedophilia as a significant social problem. However, the *Guardian*'s claims on scales are moderate compared to the *NOTW*'s, and the *Guardian* continues to voice counter-claims emphasising the rarity of paedophile incidents (understood as stranger danger). The *NOTW* can indeed be accused of creating an atmosphere of fear by constantly using large figures to construct paedophilia as a problem of *huge* proportions, and by deploying linguistic strategies which make readers feel personally at risk. But if numbers are an easy way of constructing an issue as a serious problem they are also an obvious one, resulting in a considerable degree of dispute and rejection. Numbers and numeric claims in this focus group study have been far more contested than discursive figures, presumably because they are more obviously social constructions and claims rather than 'truths'. While most focus group participants considered paedophilia a significant social problem, the *NOTW*'s most extreme constructions of paedophilia as a ubiquitous threat were only accepted by those participants whose direct experiences fitted in with these claims, i.e. where there was a cumulative and confirmative effect.

Numbers and statistics can help make sense of attitudes and practices regarding paedophiles, but explanatory insights are mostly rooted in the discourses and discursive figures which produce our understanding of paedophilia. There are multiple reasons for social reactions to paedophilia, marked by interest and emotiveness, all of which are partial accounts rather than complete models of causation. The dynamics between the discourse of innocence, the process of sacralisation and paedophilia as a sexual crime are one explanation. Sacralisation generates a societal predisposition to be concerned about risks to children, and sexual crimes generally generate much interest and outrage (Greer 2003). According to Foucault (1978) sexual crimes appear particularly grave because sexuality is seen as the essence and truth of a person. In the case of paedophilia the connection of sacralisation and sexuality results in more than a 'doubling effect' of interest and concern. The discourse of innocence essentially defines children as asexual, which renders *sexual* crimes against *children* 'unnatural' and truly horrific. Interest and indignation multiply, and this effect is further compounded by the opportunities for moralising and moral rhetoric which paedophilia offers. The moral quality of the discourse of innocence means that to speak on behalf of children is seen as moral, decent and caring. Children's charities, the media and others often claim that society's concern with paedophilia indicates care and morality, but this claim is exposed as misconceived. In fact, the very tendency to equate expressions of outrage with morality perpetuates the paedophilia controversy by facilitating moralising.

The production of 'the paedophile' as a discursive figure implicates a process of categorisation. Paedophiles are portrayed as a particular type or category, a type which is othered (paedophiles are portrayed as different from 'normal society') and demonised (paedophiles are constructed as beyond humanity). As instances of a type, paedophiles are recognisable. The process of categorisation is, however, combined with the opposite process of individualisation–universalisation. Here, the media and focus group participants claim that any individual could be a paedophile, that paedophiles are unrecognisable. Paedophiles are therefore simultaneously constructed as knowable and unknowable, types and individuals, demons and human. These contradictory processes and claims are central to explaining the potential of the figure of 'the paedophile' to incite fear in two ways. First, its dangerousness is rooted in its ambiguity and contradictoriness rather than the simple negativity of the folk devil (Cohen 1972). What makes paedophiles so dangerous is the fact that they are constructed as both normal and abnormal, rational and irrational, evil and cunning, human and animal, close and remote. Second, this highly dangerous figure is universalised, and can therefore be suspected anywhere. The complexity of the incitement of fear is further revealed through the twin functions which the twin processes of individualisation–universalisation and categorisation perform: they fuel fears (by creating a highly dangerous universal figure), and contain fears (by locating danger in 'the other'). Hence, we can hypothesise that society constructs 'the paedophile' as such a terrifying and ubiquitous figure because it enjoys the fuelling of fear *within limits*.

The twin processes are reflected again in the governance of paedophilia. Being both knowable and unknowable, the discursive figure of 'the paedophile' enables as well as disables governance. It makes regulative practices easy by providing specific instructions, and renders the same practices ineffective through notions of paedophiles being incurable and unrecognisable. These dynamics of governance result in a paradoxical situation where the regulation of paedophilia increases yet has little impact on concerns. We cannot govern our way out of fear, and as governance is a key social mechanism for dealing with risks and problems, concerns continue. Further, the paedophilia controversy results not only in a failure to reassure through governance but in a crisis of governance. It exposes the incoherence and limits of neo-liberalism as a philosophy and political strategy, and produces an extensive critique of the government. This critique culminates in disputes between the media, the wider public and the government over the fundamental right to govern, producing a legitimation crisis which may be another reason why paedophiles have become subject to so much persisting interest, concern and outrage.

Media discourses

In attempts to make sense of social reactions to paedophilia nuances have been lost for the sake of generalisations, as far as both the media and relationships between the media and focus groups are concerned. The *NOTW* and the *Guardian* are both involved in the construction of 'the paedophile' as a discursive figure and category of person, and they rely on the same discourses. However, there are differences which mean that 'the paedophile' as constructed in the *NOTW* is not exactly the same as in the *Guardian*. Differences concern the frequencies with which discourses are used, the amount of oversimplification and stereotyping involved, and the choices made between similar discourses. Simply put, while 'the paedophile' in the *NOTW* emerges as a perverted, cunning and evil devil which needs to be locked up for life, in the *Guardian* it appears as a cunning, deviant and abnormal person with *some*, if limited and uncertain, possibilities of control. While both newspapers create 'the paedophile' as a figure with the same habits and characteristics, the figure in the *Guardian* is less of a demon, more human, and retains a (small) chance to be returned to some kind of 'normality'.

Generally, the *Guardian* in comparison with the *NOTW* proves to be less sensational, more liberal and more complex, and provides a much greater range of voices. It offers a slightly different but not radically alternative way of understanding issues around paedophilia, i.e. the differences do not mount up to the provision of a liberal discourse which is opposed to the populist one. The lack of an alternative, liberal discourse is indicated by the *Guardian*'s involvement in the construction of the figure of 'the paedophile' and its understanding of child sexual abuse through this figure. It further supports various punitive legal measure and solutions which are incompatible with a liberal perspective. Paedophilia is a social problem capable of generating considerable consensus in that paedophiles are widely abhorred, and this position is reflected in the *Guardian*'s recent use of tabloid terminology to describe paedophiles, i.e. a language which the paper still considers unacceptable in relation to other stereotyped social groups. In this context of converging terminologies the prospects for the emergence of a liberal discourse seem rather bleak.

This research has produced mixed results regarding the power of the media to shape popular understanding and practices through discourses. On the one hand, there is considerable power as focus group participants often understand issues around paedophilia through the same discourses as the media and embrace the figure of 'the paedophile'. Through this figure the media are able to shape practices, such as parental governance. On the other hand, media power is limited as some individuals ignore or actively reject certain aspects or implications of discourses. For instance, the Internet, which the media represent as a major problem in relation to paedophiles, largely fails to incite concerns as its virtual nature renders any risks 'unreal'. Media impact is also shaped by context factors such as personal circumstances, subject positions and direct experiences. In any case, the power of the media clearly lies not in its

ability to pass on messages directly but in its ability to shape understanding through popularising certain discourses which provide
interpretatve frameworks and ways of understanding. The idea of
'the paedophile' as a distinct figure is not challenged, even if particular aspects of it might be disputed, and paedophilia and child
sexual abuse are widely understood though this discursive figure.
Similarly, the discourses of pathology or evil are so widely (re)pro-
duced that we have to talk and think about paedophiles in terms of
evil and pathology, even if only to reject these characteristics.

Meanings matter

Research primarily concerned with discourses and meanings is often
regarded with some suspicion in the social sciences. Especially on a
topic like paedophilia social research tends to be policy driven (e.g.
Silverman and Wilson 2002; Taylor and Quayle 2003), and there
are demands for 'practical' implications such as measures for
improving child protection. Of course the discursive and the 'practical' are not mutually exclusive spaces; many 'practical' critiques
have been levelled at the way in which paedophilia is currently
understood.

First of all, it produces several myths. The source of danger is mis-
construed because, as La Fontaine (1990) has pointed out, most
child sexual abuse takes place in the family and is not perpetrated
by strangers. Further, the offender, i.e. 'the paedophile', is incor-
rectly 'othered'. Available research has repeatedly suggested that
those who sexually abuse children are a diverse group (apart from
being predominantly male) (Eldridge 2000; Fisher and Beech 2004),
a group which is not significantly different from non-abusers in
terms of personality, psychological make-up or social interaction
(Howitt 1995; Thomas 2000). Second, conceptualising child sexual
abuse through the figure of 'the paedophile' individualises a social
problem, which obscures important social factors and renders the
solutions society envisages narrow, misguided and ineffective
(Kitzinger 1999). Child protection is often not the outcome. For
instance, if family members rather than strangers are the main
source of child sexual abuse then new government laws against
strangers 'grooming' children for sexual abuse will have limited
impact. So much for equating increased concern and action with
care and protection. Third, by focusing on degendered dangerous

strangers it becomes possible not only to ignore the role of gender and hegemonic masculinity but also to reinforce the latter. As paedophiles are 'othered', 'normal' men continue to be seen as entirely separate from them and can continue in their role of protectors of women and children (Cowburn and Dominelli 2001). Fourth, my research has clearly shown that parents are encouraged and pressured to regulate extensively their children's lives, which end up significantly restricted and supervised. Again, protection is the desired but unlikely outcome considering the misconception of the source of danger.

If these myths and misconceptions are known, why and how are they perpetuated? Only a focus on meanings and discourses can offer answers. The understanding of paedophilia revolves around interconnected discursive figures, which are simplistic, stereotypical and often oppositional in their constructions. These figures enable the telling of a black-and-white story in which paedophiles are thoroughly evil and manipulative, children inherently weak and vulnerable, parents 'naturally' the safe protectors, and strangers the source of danger. They facilitate and produce the misconceptions and myths outlined above, for instance that the figure of 'the paedophile' is a stranger and a distinct type who bears little relation to other individuals in society. 'The paedophile' is, in my opinion, not degendered but male; however, his gender is not actively recognised as a feature of the type. Maleness, unlike characteristics such as cunning, does not play a role in the definition of what makes a paedophile. Hence understanding and explanations of paedophilia are located not in gender but in 'the paedophile', who, as a distinct type, has nothing in common with any 'normal' person, male or female. In this scenario, traditional roles such as the male protector can certainly continue.

Discursive figures not only facilitate misconceptions such as the child sexual abuser as a dangerous, abnormal stranger, but also help maintain paedophil*es* as a social problem. Paedophiles can only be represented as a major threat because 'the paedophile' is constructed as an extremely dangerous 'other' *and* universal, and children are portrayed as totally helpless. This is not to suggest that child sexual abuse is not a serious or significant problem. Feminists (e.g. Driver and Droisen 1989) have long emphasised the widespread and 'normal' nature of child sexual abuse, especially within the family, which is grounded in the power structures of male dominance.

Conceptual shifts from child sexual abuse to 'the paedophile' (Corby 2000) have retained feminist claims on scales, but reversed their analyses on the nature and causes of child sexual abuse. Hence discursive figures have to be challenged, not just to expose misconceptions but to reveal the contradictions inherent in maintaining paedophiles as a large-scale problem perpetrated by abnormal individuals. However, these figures are deeply entrenched and widely (re)produced. For instance, the figure of the innocent child has proved resistant to experiential and research-based challenges, and the figures of the stranger paedophile or the protective parent can simply be assumed as known 'truths'. It is precisely the deep entrenchment of these discursive figures which enables myths and contradictions to persist in the face of trends and incidents undermining them.

Thus representations, discourses and meanings are central to paedophilia, and without them we simply cannot make sense of some key questions. These include the perpetuation of misconceptions, reasons for emotive concerns and why measures taken to combat the social problem do not work to diminish anxieties. This last question puzzles social policy research, which aims to improve governmental measures for dealing with paedophiles and thereby reduce public concerns. Only discursive analyses can shed light on this conundrum by revealing that we cannot legislate our way out of fear because new laws and social policy measures are by definition futile. Their futility is rooted in the discursive figure of 'the paedophile' which renders ineffective the very regulative practices which it enables. These insights elude a policy-oriented approach because it takes for granted the object of its enquiry, i.e. paedophilia and its figures and discourses.

While the revelation of discourses is central to a critique, there also needs to be a recognition that representations, meanings and discourses do not simply appear. We, as individuals and social groups within society, are the (re)producers of discourses through our opinions, actions and stories; this is hopefully what this book has begun to show by directing research at multiple levels. Acknowledging our own role in the construction of discourses and representations would be a first step towards confronting uncomfortable issues such as the motivations of our involvement. This would make it difficult to argue for paedophilia as the last 'natural' social problem, and to equate child regulation and paedophile condemnation with care, altruism and morality. However, this process is likely to be a difficult and long one, considering that even traditionally liberal and academic institutions, such as the *Guardian*, the natural sciences (see Davis 2005) and even parts of the social sciences (e.g. Livingstone 2001; Quayle and Taylor 2002; Silverman and Wilson 2002), have largely accepted the discourses and discursive figures on which the paedophilia controversy is built.

Appendix: focus group participants

Focus group 1: basic biographical details*

Name	Age category	Gender	Ethnicity	Occupation	Social class
Abi	35–9	Female	White British	College student, access course	Upper working class
Amy	20–4	Female	White British	College student, access course	Upper working class
Jack	35–9	Male	Black British	College student, access course	Upper working class
James	20–4	Male	White British	College student, access course	Upper working class
Kerry	35–9	Female	Black British	College student, access course	Upper working class
Miles	30–4	Male	White British	College student, access course	Upper working class
Ravi	20–4	Male	Asian British	College student, access course	Upper working class

* All information self-reported and self-defined except for the category of social class, which was derived from the Registrar-General's social class classification (Crompton 1998).

Focus group 1: parenthood and media consumption

Name	Number of children	Age category of children (respective numbers in brackets)	Newspapers read (ranked in terms of frequency)	Frequency of reading (all newspapers)
Abi	4	5–10 (2) 14–16 (1) 17–20 (1)	*Daily Mail/ Mail on Sunday* *MEN* *Metro*	Daily
Amy	None	N/A	*Sun* *The Times/Sunday Times*	4–6 times a week
Jack	None	N/A	*Sun* *MEN* *Guardian*	Daily
James	None	N/A	*Sun* *MEN* *Metro* *NOTW* *Daily/ Sunday Mirror* *Daily/Sunday Star* *Guardian* *Independent/ Independent on Sunday*	Daily
Kerry	2	Under 5 (1) 5–10 (1)	*MEN** *Metro*	2–3 times a week
Miles	4	5–10 (1) 11–13 (2) 14–16 (1)	*Sun* *NOTW* *MEN* *Daily/ Sunday Mirror* *Daily/ Sunday Telegraph*	Daily
Ravi	None	N/A	*Daily/ Sunday Mirror* *Daily Mail/Mail on Sunday* *MEN* *Guardian* *Observer*	Daily

* MEN (*Manchester Evening News*)

Appendix

Focus group 2: basic biographical details*

Name	Age category	*Gender*	Ethnicity	Occupation	Social class
Celia	30–4	Female	White British	Lecturer	Upper middle class
Christine	35–9	Female	White British	Secretary	Working class
Ellie	20–4	Female	White British	University student, undergraduate	Middle class
Emily	40+	Female	White British	Secretary	Working class
Hannah	30–4	Female	White Cypriot	University student, postgraduate	Middle class
Helen	35–9	Female	White British	University student, undergraduate	Middle class
Kate	40+	Female	White British	Secretary	Working class
Pilar	25–9	Female	White Hispanic	University student, postgraduate	Middle class
Rachel	40+	Female	White British	University student, undergraduate	Middle class
Vic	30–4	Female	White British	Secretary	Working class

* All information self-reported and self-defined except for the category of social class, which was derived from the Registrar-General's social class classification (Crompton 1998).

Focus group 2: parenthood and media consumption

Name	Number of children	Age category of children (respective numbers in brackets)	Newspapers read (ranked in terms of frequency)	Frequency of reading (all newspapers)
Celia	1	Under 5	*Guardian* *Times Higher Education Supplement*	2–3 times a week
Christine	2	5–10 (2)	*Express/ Sunday Express* *Daily/ Sunday Mirror*	4–6 times a week
Ellie	1	Under 5	*Guardian* MEN *Observer* *Metro*	2–3 times a week
Emily	2	5–10 (1) 14–16 (1)	*Daily Mail/ Mail on Sunday* MEN	Daily
Hannah	1	Under 5	*Guardian* *Observer*	2–3 times a week
Helen	1	Under 5	*Guardian*	Once a week
Kate	1	11–13	*Daily/ Sunday Mirror* MEN	Daily
Pilar	1	Under 5	MEN*	Once a month
Rachel	2	20+ (2)	*Guardian* *Observer* *Independent/ Independent on Sunday* MEN	Daily
Vic	2	Under 5 (1) 11–13 (1)	Local paper *NOTW* *Daily/ Sunday Mirror*	2–3 times a week

* MEN (*Manchester Evening News*)

Focus group 3: basic biographical details*

Name	Age category	Gender	Ethnicity	Occupation	Housing	Social class
Beth	30–4	Female	White British	Housewife	Privately rented, Rusholme	Lower working class
Claire	25–9	Female	White British	Housewife	Council estate, Fallowfield	Lower working class
Donna	40+	Female	White Irish	Unemployed	Council estate, Rusholme	Lower working class
Dorothy	40+	Female	Black Other	Unemployed	Council estate, Rusholme	Lower working class
Fiona	35–9	Female	White British	Group leader	Owner–occupier of a house in Rusholme	Middle class
Lisa	40+	Female	White British	Housewife	Council estate, Rusholme	Lower working class
Pat	30–4	Female	White British	Unemployed	Council estate, Rusholme	Lower working class
Sarah	25–9	Female	Mixed Heritage	Housewife	Council estate, Rusholme	Lower working class
Sinead	20–4	Female	White Irish	Housewife	Privately rented, Rusholme	Lower working class
Tanya	35–9	Female	Mixed Heritage	Unemployed	Not known	Lower working class

* All information self-reported and self-defined except for the category of social class, which was derived from the Registrar-General's social class classification (Crompton 1998). Information on type and area of housing was volunteered in discussions and has been included because it supports social class classification. Rusholme and Fallowfield are relatively deprived inner-city areas in Manchester.

Focus group 3: parenthood and media consumption

Name	Number of children	Age category of children (respective numbers in brackets)	Newspapers read (ranked in terms of frequency)	Frequency of reading (all newspapers)
Beth	2	5–10 (1) 11–13 (1)	*Sun* *NOTW* *MEN*	2–3 times a week
Claire	3	Under 5 (2) 5–10 (1)	*Daily/ Sunday Mirror* Local papers	Once a week
Donna	3	Under 5 (1) 5–10 (1) 20+ (1)	*Express/ Sunday Express* *MEN*	2–3 times a week
Dorothy	1	20+	*Daily/Sunday Mirror*	Once a week
Fiona	2	Under 5 (1) 5–10 (1)	*Guardian* *Observer* *MEN*	4–6 times a week
Lisa	3	Under 5 (1) 5–10 (2)	*Sun* *NOTW* *MEN*	Daily
Pat	3	Under 5 (1) 5–10 (1) 11–13 (1)	*MEN*	Daily
Sarah	3	Under 5 (3)	*MEN*	Once a week
Sinead	1	Under 5	*Sun* *NOTW* *Daily/ Sunday Mirror* *Daily/ Sunday Star* *MEN**	Daily
Tanya	3	Under 5 (1) 5–10 (2)	*Sun* *NOTW* *MEN*	2–3 times a week

* MEN (*Manchester Evening News*)

Bibliography

Adkins, L. (2001) 'Risk cultures, self-reflexivity and the making of sexual hierarchies', *Body and Society*, 7:1, 35–55.

Ahmed, S. (2000) *Strange Encounters: Embodied Others in Post-Coloniality*. London: Routledge.

Alexander, J. C. (1996) 'Critical reflections on "reflexive modernisation" ', *Theory, Culture and Society*, 13:4, 133–8.

Ariès, P. (1962) *Centuries of Childhood*. London: Jonathan Cape.

Ashenden, S. (2002) 'Policing perversion: the contemporary governance of paedophilia', *Cultural Values*, 6:1, 197–222.

Ashenden, S. (2004) *Governing Child Sexual Abuse: Negotiating the Boundaries of Public and Private, Law and Science*. London: Routledge.

Bagley, C. (1997) *Children, Sex and Social Policy: Humanistic Solutions for Problems of Child Sexual Abuse*. Aldershot: Avebury.

Bauman, Z. (1997) *Postmodernity and its Discontents*. Cambridge: Polity.

Bauman, Z. (2001) 'The social construction of ambivalence', in P. Beilharz (ed.) *The Bauman Reader*. Oxford: Blackwell.

Beck, U. (1992) *Risk Society: Towards a New Modernity*. London: Sage.

Beck, U. (2000) 'Risk society revisited: theory, politics and research programmes', in B. Adam, U. Beck and J. Van Loon (eds) *The Risk Society and Beyond: Critical Issues for Social Theory*. London: Sage.

Bell, V. (1993a) *Interrogating Incest: Feminism, Foucault and the Law*. London: Routledge.

Bell, V. (1993b) 'Governing childhood: neo-liberalism and the law', *Economy and Society*, 22:3, 390–405.

Bell, V. (2002) 'The vigilant(e) parent and the paedophile – the *News of the World* campaign 2000 and the contemporary governmentality of child sexual abuse', *Feminist Theory*, 3:1, 83–102.

Benedict, H. (1992) *Virgin or Vamp: How the Press Covers Sex Crimes*. Oxford: Oxford University Press.

Bennett, R. (21 November 2003) 'Sacrifice of trial by jury plans saves justice bill', *The Times*, p. 17.

Best, J. (1990) *Threatened Children: Rhetoric and Concern about Child Victims*. Chicago: University of Chicago Press.

Bingham, N., G. Valentine and S. L. Holloway (1999) 'Where do you want to go tomorrow? Connecting children and the internet', *Environment and Planning D: Society and Space*, 17, 655–72.

Bloor, M., J. Frankland, M. Thomas and K. Robson (2001) *Focus Groups in Social Research*. London: Sage.

Boyer, R. (1996) 'State and the market – a new engagement for the twenty-first century?', in R. Boyer and D. Drache (eds) *States Against Markets: The Limits of Globalisation*. London: Routledge.

Buckingham, D. (2001) 'Electronic child abuse? Rethinking the media's effects on children', in M. Barker and J. Petley (eds) *Ill Effects: The Media/Violence Debate*. London: Routledge.

Butler, J. (1993) *Bodies that Matter: On the Discursive Limits of 'Sex'*. London: Routledge.

Campbell, B. (1988) *Unofficial Secrets: Child Sexual Abuse – The Cleveland Case*. London: Virago.

Card, R. (2004) *Sexual Offences: The New Law*. Bristol: Jordans.

Carrier, J. G. (1997) 'Introduction', in J. G. Carrier (ed.) *Meanings of the Market: The Free Market in Western Culture*. Oxford: Berg.

Carter, H. (24 September 2003) 'Microsoft chatrooms to close after abuse fear', *Guardian*, p. 1.

Carter, H. (1 December 2003) 'Paedophile found beaten to death at home', *Guardian*, p. 6.

Chaplin, E. (1994) *Sociology and Visual Representation*. London: Routledge.

Christensen, P. H. (2000) 'Childhood and the cultural construction of vulnerable bodies', in A. Prout (ed.) *The Body, Childhood and Society*. Basingstoke: Macmillan.

Clixby, H. (6 May 2005) 'Life sentence for "Savage" murderer', *Journal* (Newcastle).

Cobley, C. (2000) *Sex Offenders: Law, Policy and Practice*. Bristol: Jordans.

Cobley, C. (2005) *Sex Offenders: Law, Policy and Practice*. Bristol: Jordans.

Cohen, S. (1972) *Folk Devils and Moral Panics: The Creation of the Mods and Rockers*. London: MacGibbon and Kee.

Colclough, C. (1991) 'Structuralism versus neo-liberalism: an introduction', in C. Colclough and J. Manor (eds) *States or Markets? Neo-Liberalism and the Development Policy Debate*. Oxford: Clarendon Press.

Collier, R. (2001) 'Dangerousness, popular knowledge and the criminal law: a case study of the paedophile as a sociocultural phenomenon', in P. Alldridge and C. Brants (eds) *Personal Autonomy, the Private Sphere and the Criminal Law*. Oxford: Hart.

Corby, B. (2000) *Child Abuse: Towards a Knowledge Base*. Buckingham: Open University Press.

Cowburn, M. and L. Dominelli (2001) 'Masking hegemonic masculinity: reconstructing the paedophile as the dangerous stranger', *British Journal of Social Work*, 31, 399–415.

Craig, T. and J. Petley (2001) 'Invasion of the internet abusers – marketing fears about the information superhighway', in M. Barker and J. Petley (eds) *Ill Effects: The Media/Violence Debate*. London: Routledge.

Critcher, C. (2000a) 'Madness in their methods: moral panics and the mass media', professorial lecture, Sheffield Hallam University.

Critcher, C. (2000b) 'Government, media and moral crisis: paedophilia in the British press in the summer of 2000', Naples University, 'Communication in Crisis' conference.

Critcher, C. (2003) *Moral Panics and the Media*. Buckingham: Open University Press.

Crompton, R. (1998) *Class and Stratification: An Introduction to Current Debates*. Cambridge: Polity.

Curran, J. and J. Seaton (1997) *Power Without Responsibility: The Press and Broadcasting in Britain* (5th edition). London: Routledge.

Daily Express (13 January 2004) 'Net fuels surge in child porn', p. 2.

David, M. E. (1980) *The State, the Family and Education*. London: Routledge and Kegan Paul.

Davies, B. and R. Harré (2001) 'Positioning: the discursive production of selves', in M. Wetherell, S. Taylor and S. J. Yates (eds) *Discourse Theory and Practice: A Reader*. London: Sage.

Davin, A. (1999) 'What is a child?', in A. Fletcher and S. Hussey (eds) *Childhood in Question: Children, Parents and the State*. Manchester: Manchester University Press.

Davis, J. E. (2005) *Accounts of Innocence: Sexual Abuse, Trauma, and the Self*. London: University of Chicago Press.

Dean, M. (1998) 'Risk, calculable and incalculable', *Soziale Welt*, 49, 25–42.

Dean, M. (1999a) *Governmentality: Power and Rule in Modern Society*. London: Sage.

Dean, M. (1999b) 'Risk, calculable and incalculable', in D. Lupton (ed.) *Risk and Sociocultural Theory: New Directions and Perspectives*. Cambridge: Cambridge University Press.

Dingwall, R., J. Eekelaar and T. Murray (1983) *The Protection of Children: State Intervention and Family Life*. Oxford: Blackwell.

Donzelot, J. (1979) *The Policing of Families: Welfare Versus the State*. London: Hutchinson.

Douglas, M. (1992) *Risk and Blame: Essays in Cultural Theory*. London: Routledge.

Douglas, M. and A. Wildavsky (1982) *Risk and Culture: An Essay on the Selection of Technological and Environmental Dangers*. Berkeley: University of California Press.

Driver, E. and A. Droisen (1989) *Child Sexual Abuse: Feminist Perspectives*. London: Macmillan.

Edwards, J. (2000) *Born and Bred: Idioms of Kinship and New Reproductive Technologies in England*. Oxford: Oxford University Press.

Eldridge, H. (2000) 'Patterns of sex offending and strategies for effective assessment and intervention', in C. Itzin (ed.) *Home Truths about Child Sexual Abuse: Influencing Policy and Practice: A Reader*. London: Routledge.

Eldridge, J. (1999) 'Risk, society and the media: now you see it, now you don't', in G. Philo (ed.) *Message Received: Glasgow Media Group Research 1993–1998*. Harlow: Longman.

Evans, M. and C. M. Butkus (1997) 'Regulating the emergent: cyberporn and the traditional media', *Media International Australia*, 85, 62–9.

Fairclough, N. (1989) *Language and Power*. London: Longman.

Fairclough, N. (1995) *Media Discourse*. London: Edward Arnold.

Fairclough, N. (1999) 'Linguistic and intertextual analysis in discourse analysis', in A. Jaworski and N. Coupland (eds) *The Discourse Reader*. London: Routledge.

Fairclough, N. (2003) *Analysing Discourse: Textual Analysis for Social Research*. London: Routledge.

Fairclough, N. and R. Wodak (1997) 'Critical discourse analysis', in T. A. van Dijk (ed.). *Discourse Studies: A Multidisciplinary Introduction. Vol. 2: Discourse as Social Interaction*. London: Sage.

Fisher, D. D. and A. R. Beech (2004) 'Adult male sex offenders', in H. Kemshall and G. McIvor (eds) *Managing Sex Offender Risk*. London: Jessica Kingsley.

Ford, R. (20 November 2002) 'Blunkett sweeps away Victorian anti-gay sex laws', *The Times*, p. 4.

Foucault, M. (1978) *The History of Sexuality: An Introduction. Vol. 1*. Harmondsworth: Penguin.

Foucault, M. (1979) *Discipline and Punish: The Birth of the Prison*. Harmondsworth: Penguin.

Foucault, M. (1988) 'The dangerous individual', in L. D. Kritzman (ed.) *Michel Foucault: Politics, Philosophy and Culture*. London: Routledge.

Fowler, R. (1985) 'Power', in T. A. Van Dijk (ed.) *Handbook of Discourse Analysis: Discourse Analysis and Society. Vol. 4*. London: Academic Press.

Fowler, R. (1991) *Language in the News: Discourse and Ideology in the Press*. London: Routledge.

Frank, T. (2001) *One Market Under God: Extreme Capitalism, Market Populism and the End of Economic Democracy*. London: Secker and Warburg.

Frankland, J. and M. Bloor (1999) 'Some issues arising in the systematic analysis of focus group materials', in R. S. Barbour and J. Kitzinger (eds) *Developing Focus Group Research: Politics, Theory and Practice*. London: Sage.

Frey, J. H. and A. Fontana (1993) 'The group interview in social research', in D. L. Morgan (ed.) *Successful Focus Groups: Advancing the State of the Art*. London: Sage.

Furedi, F. (1997) *The Culture of Fear: Risk Taking and the Morality of Low Expectation*. London: Cassell.

Garland, D. (1999) ' "Governmentality' and the problem of crime', in R. Smandych (ed.) *Governable Places: Readings on Governmentality and Crime Control*. Aldershot: Ashgate Dartmouth.

Giddens, A. (1990) *The Consequences of Modernity*. Cambridge: Polity.

Giddens, A. (1991) *Modernity and Self-Identity: Self and Society in the Late Modern Age*. Cambridge: Polity.

Giddens, A. (1992) *The Transformation of Intimacy: Sexuality, Love and Eroticism in Modern Societies*. Cambridge: Polity.

Gilbert, N. (ed.) (1993) *Researching Social Life*. London: Sage.

Gilman, S. L. (1988) *Disease and Representation: Images of Illness from Madness to AIDS*. Ithaca, NY: Cornell University Press.

Goldblatt, D. (1996) *Social Theory and the Environment*. Cambridge: Polity.

Goode, E. and N. Ben-Yehuda (1994) *Moral Panics: The Social Construction of Deviance*. Oxford: Blackwell.

Gordon, C. (1991) 'Governmental rationality: an introduction', in G. Burchell, C. Gordon and P. Miller (eds) *The Foucault Effect: Studies in Governmentality*. London: Harvester Wheatsheaf.

Graddol, D. (1994) 'The visual accomplishment of factuality', in D. Graddol and O. Boyd-Barrett (eds) *Media Texts: Authors and Readers*. Clevedon: Open University Press.

Green, J. and L. Hart (1999) 'The impact of context on data', in R. S. Barbour and J. Kitzinger (eds) *Developing Focus Group Research: Politics, Theory and Practice*. London: Sage.

Greenslade, R. (1 May 1997) 'The election: mediawatch: the press. Taming paper tigers, but for how long', *Guardian*, p. 19.

Greer, C. (2003) *Sex Crime and the Media: Sex Offending and the Press in a Divided Society*. Cullompton: Willan.

Grubin, D. (2004) 'The risk assessment of sex offenders', in H. Kemshall and G. McIvor (eds) *Managing Sex Offender Risk*. London: Jessica Kingsley.

Guardian (19 April 1997) 'May Day and great expectations', p. 20.

Guardian (6 June 2001) 'Give them a second term', p. 23.

Guardian (3 May 2005) 'Once more with feeling: general election', p. 19.

Guardian (5 December 2005) 'Civil partnerships: straight choice for all', p. 28.

Hall, S. (1997) *Representation: Cultural Representations and Signifying Practices*. London: Sage.

Hall, S. (2001) 'Foucault: power, knowledge and discourse', in M. Wetherell, S. Taylor and S. J. Yates (eds) *Discourse Theory and Practice: A Reader*. London: Sage.

Hansen, A. (1998) 'Media audiences: focus group interviewing', in A. Hansen, S. Cottle, R. Negrine and C. Newbold (eds) *Mass Communication Research Methods*. Basingstoke: Macmillan.

Hendrick, H. (1997) 'Constructions and reconstructions of British childhood: an interpretive survey, 1800 to the present', in A. James and A. Prout (eds) *Constructing and Reconstructing Childhood: Contemporary Issues in the Sociological Study of Childhood*. London: Falmer Press.

Herbert, I. (23 March 2005) 'Death by gossip', *Independent*, pp. 1–2.

Hier, S. P. (2003) 'Risk and panic in late modernity: implications of the converging sites of social anxiety', *British Journal of Sociology*, 54:1, 3–20.

Holloway, S. and G. Valentine (2003) *Cyberkids: Children in the Information Age*. London: Routledge Falmer.

Hollway, W. and T. Jefferson (1997) 'The risk society in an age of anxiety: situating fear of crime', *British Journal of Sociology*, 48:2, 255–66.

Hornsby-Smith, M. (1993) 'Gaining access', in N. Gilbert (ed.) *Researching Social Life*. London: Sage.

Howitt, D. (1995) *Paedophiles and Sexual Offences Against Children*, Chichester: John Wiley.

Hutchings, P. J. (2001) *The Criminal Spectre in Law, Literature and Aesthetics: Incriminating Subjects*. London: Routledge.

Jackson, L. A. (1999) 'Family, community and the regulation of child sexual abuse', in A. Fletcher and S. Hussey (eds) *Childhood in Question: Children, Parents and the State*. Manchester: Manchester University Press.

Jackson, S. (1982) *Childhood and Sexuality*. Oxford: Blackwell.

Jackson, S. and S. Scott (1999) 'Risk anxiety and the social construction of childhood', in D. Lupton (ed.) *Risk and Sociocultural Theory: New Directions and Perspectives*. Cambridge: Cambridge University Press.

James, A., C. Jenks and A. Prout (1998) *Theorising Childhood*. Cambridge: Polity.

Jancovich, M. (1992) *Horror*. London: Batsford.

Jenkins, P. (1992) *Intimate Enemies: Moral Panics in Contemporary Great Britain*. New York: Aldine de Gruyter.

Jenkins, P. (1998) *Moral Panic: Changing Concepts of the Child Molester in Modern America*. London and New Haven, CT: Yale University Press.

Jenks, C. (1996) *Childhood*. London: Sage.

Jordanova, L. (2000) *Defining Features: Scientific and Medical Portraits 1660–2000*. London: Reaktion Books.

Jucker, A. (1992) *Social Stylistics: Syntactic Variation in British Newspapers*. Berlin: Mouton de Gruyter

Kabeer, N. and J. Humphrey (1991) 'Neo-liberalism, gender and the limits of the market', in C. Colclough and J. Manor (eds) *States or Markets? Neo-Liberalism and the Development Policy Debate*. Oxford: Clarendon Press.

Kelly, L. (1996) 'Weasel words: paedophiles and the cycle of abuse', *Trouble and Strife*, 33, 44–9.

Kempe, R. S. and C. H. Kempe (1978) *Child Abuse*. London: Open Books.

Kemshall, H. and G. McIvor (2004) 'Sex offenders: policy and legislative developments', in H. Kemshall and G. McIvor (eds) *Managing Sex Offender Risk*. London: Jessica Kingsley.

Kerr, A. and S. Cunningham-Burley (2000) 'On ambivalence and risk: reflexive modernity and the new human genetics', *Sociology*, 34:2, 283–304.

Kincaid, J. R. (1998) *Erotic Innocence: The Culture of Child Molesting*. London: Duke University Press.

Kitzinger, J. (1994) 'The methodology of focus groups: the importance of interaction between research participants', *Sociology of Health and Illness*, 16:1, 103–21.

Kitzinger, J. (1997) 'Who are you kidding? Children, power and the struggle against sexual abuse', in A. James and A. Prout (eds) *Constructing and Reconstructing Childhood: Contemporary Issues in the Sociological Study of Childhood*. London: Falmer Press.

Kitzinger, J. (1999) 'The ultimate neighbour from hell? Stranger danger and the media framing of paedophiles', in B. Franklin (ed.) *Social Policy, the Media and Misrepresentation*. London: Routledge.

Kitzinger, J. (2004) *Framing Abuse: Media Influence and Public Understanding of Sexual Violence against Children*. London: Pluto.

Kitzinger, J. and R. S. Barbour (1999) 'Introduction: the challenge and promise of focus groups', in R. S. Barbour and J. Kitzinger (eds) *Developing Focus Group Research: Politics, Theory and Practice*. London: Sage.

Kitzinger, J. and C. Farquhar (1999) 'The analytical potential of "sensitive moments" in focus group discussions', in R. S. Barbour and J. Kitzinger (eds) *Developing Focus Group Research: Politics, Theory and Practice*. London: Sage.

Kitzinger, J. and P. Skidmore (1995) *Child Sexual Abuse and the Media*. Summary report to the ESRC.

Kohler Riessman, C. (1993) *Narrative Analysis*. London: Sage.

Knodel, J. (1993) 'The design and analysis of focus group studies', in D. L. Morgan (ed.) *Successful Focus Groups: Advancing the State of the Art*. London: Sage.

Kress, G. (1983) 'Linguistic and ideological transformation in news reporting', in H. Davis and P. Walton (eds) *Language, Image, Media*. Oxford: Blackwell.

Kress, G. (1985) 'Ideological structures in discourse', in T. A. Van Dijk (ed.) *Handbook of Discourse Analysis: Discourse Analysis and Society. Vol. 4*. London: Academic Press.

Kress, G. and T. Van Leeuwen (1996) *Reading Images: The Grammar of Visual Design*. London: Routledge.

Kress, G. and T. Van Leeuwen (2001) *Multimodal Discourse: The Modes and Media of Contemporary Communication*. London: Arnold.

Krueger, R. A. (1998a) *Developing Questions for Focus Group Research*. London: Sage.

Krueger, R. A. (1998b) *Analysing and Reporting Focus Group Results*. London: Sage.

La Fontaine, J. (1990) *Child Sexual Abuse*. Cambridge: Polity.

Lansdown, G. (1994) 'Children's rights', in B. Mayall (ed.) *Children's Childhoods: Observed and Experienced*. London: Falmer Press.

Lash, S. (1993) 'Reflexive modernisation: the aesthetic dimension', *Theory, Culture and Society*, 10:1, 1–23.

Lash, S. (1994) 'Reflexivity and its doubles: structure, aesthetics, community', in U. Beck, A. Giddens and S. Lash (eds) *Reflexive Modernisation: Politics, Tradition and Aesthetics in the Modern Social Order*. Cambridge: Polity.

Lash, S. (2000) 'Risk culture', in B. Adam, U. Beck and J. Van Loon (eds) *The Risk Society and Beyond: Critical Issues for Social Theory*. London: Sage.

Lavalette, M. (2005) ' "In defence of childhood": against the neo-liberal assault on social life', in J. Qvortrup (ed.) *Studies in Modern Childhood: Society, Agency, Culture*. Basingstoke: Palgrave Macmillan.

Lawler, S. (2000) *Mothering the Self: Mothers, Daughters, Subjects*. London: Routledge.

Lawler, S. (2002) 'Mobs and monsters: *Independent* man meets Paulsgrove woman', *Feminist Theory*, 3:1, 103–13.

Leaning, M. (2002) 'The person we meet online', *Convergence*, 8:1, 18–27.

Lees, S. (1997) *Ruling Passions: Sexual Violence, Reputation and the Law*. Buckingham: Open University Press.

Legrand, J. and R. Robinson (1984) *The Economics of Social Problems: The Market Versus the State*. London: Macmillan.

Leys, C. (2001) *Market-Driven Politics: Neo-Liberal Democracy and the Public Interest*. London: Verso.

Livingstone, S. (2001) *Online Freedom and Safety for Children*. London: Institute for Public Policy Research, Citizens Online Research Publication No. 3.

Long, B. and B. McLachlan (2002) *The Hunt for Britain's Paedophiles*. London: Hodder and Stoughton.

Lumby, C. (1997) 'Panic attacks: old fears in a new media era', *Media International Australia*, 85, 40–6.

Lupton, D. (1999) *Risk*. London: Routledge.

MacEwan, A. (1999) *Neo-Liberalism or Democracy? Economic Strategy, Markets, and Alternatives for the 21st Century*. London: Zed Books.

Mills, S. (1997) *Discourse*. London: Routledge.

Mills, S. (2003) *Michel Foucault*. London: Routledge.

Morgan, D. L. and R. A. Krueger (1993) 'When to use focus groups and why', in D. L. Morgan (ed.) *Successful Focus Groups: Advancing the State of the Art*. London: Sage.

MORI (May–June 1998) 'The school summer holiday: at home, and going away', opinion poll commissioned by Nestlé. London: MORI

MORI (23 July 2000) 'Crime and sentencing', opinion poll commissioned by the *News of the World*. London: MORI.

MORI (20 August 2000) 'Naming and shaming', opinion poll commissioned by the *News of the World*. London: MORI.

MORI (11 December 2001) 'Rethinking crime and punishment', opinion poll commissioned by Esmee Fairbairn Foundation. London: MORI.

MORI (16 December 2001) 'Crimes against children', opinion poll commissioned by the *News of the World*. London: MORI.

MORI (19 September 2002) 'The repercussions of Soham murders', opinion poll, commissioned by the NSPCC. London: MORI.

Morley, D. (1992) *Television, Audiences and Cultural Studies*. London: Routledge.

Morrison, D. E. (1998) *Search for a Method: Focus Groups and the Development of Mass Communication Research*. Luton: University of Luton Press.

Mort, F. (1996) *Cultures of Consumption: Masculinities and Social Space in Late Twentieth-Century Britain*. London: Routledge.

Nava, M. (1988) 'Cleveland and the press: outrage and anxiety in the reporting of child sexual abuse', *Feminist Review*, 28, 103–22.

News of the World (3 June 2001) 'Delivery, delivery, delivery', p. 8.

News of the World (1 May 2005) 'Put in your X for Britain . . . and Blair', p. 6.

Oakley, A. (1972) *Sex, Gender and Society*. London: Maurice Temple Smith.

O'Connell Davidson, J. (1995) 'British sex tourists in Thailand', in M. Maynard and J. Purvis (eds) *(Hetero)sexual Politics*. London: Taylor and Francis.

O'Connell Davidson, J. (1998) *Prostitution, Power and Freedom*. Cambridge: Polity.

O'Malley, P. (1996) 'Risk and responsibility', in A. Barry, T. Osborne and N. Rose (eds) *Foucault and Political Reason: Liberalism, Neo-Liberalism and Rationalities of Government*. London: UCL Press.

Oswell, D. (1998) 'The place of "childhood" in internet content regulation: a case study of policy in the UK', *International Journal of Cultural Studies*, 1:2, 271–91.

Oswell, D. (1999) 'The dark side of cyberspace: internet content regulation and child protection', *Convergence*, 5:4, 42–62.

Parton, N. (1991) *Governing the Family: Child Care, Child Protection and the State*. London: Macmillan.

Phillips, N. and C. Hardy (2002) *Discourse Analysis: Investigating Processes of Social Construction*. London: Sage.

Philo, G. (1999) *Message Received: Glasgow Media Group Research 1993–1998*. Harlow: Longman.

Phoenix, J. and S. Oerton (2005) *Illicit and Illegal: Sex, Regulation and Social Control*. Cullompton: Willan.

Pratt, J. (1999) 'Governmentality, neo-liberalism and dangerousness', in R. Smandych (ed.) *Governable Places: Readings on Governmentality and Crime Control*. Aldershot: Ashgate Dartmouth.

Quayle, E. and M. Taylor (2002) 'Paedophiles, pornography and the internet: assessment Issues', *British Journal of Social Work*, 32, 863–75.

Qvortrup, J. (2005) 'Varieties of childhood', in J. Qvortrup (ed.) *Studies in Modern Childhood: Society, Agency, Culture*. Basingstoke: Palgrave Macmillan.

Reed, J. P. and R. S. Reed (1972) 'Status, images and consequences: once a criminal, always a criminal', in T. P. Thornberry and E. Sagarin (eds) *Images of Crime: Offenders and Victims*. New York: Praeger.

Renold, E. (2005) *Girls, Boys and Junior Sexualities: Exploring Children's Gender and Sexual Relations in the Primary School*. London: Routledge Falmer.

Riddell, P. (1998) 'Members and Millbank: the media and parliament', in J. Seaton (ed.) *Politics and the Media: Harlots and Prerogatives at the Turn of the Millennium*. Oxford: Blackwell.

Roche, J. (1996) 'The politics of children's rights', in J. Brannen and M. O'Brien (eds) *Children in Families: Research and Policy*. London: Falmer Press.

Rose, N. (1999) *Powers of Freedom: Reframing Political Thought*. Cambridge: Cambridge University Press.

Rose, N. (2000) 'Government and control', *British Journal of Criminology*, 40, 321–39.

Sampson, A. (1994) *Acts of Abuse: Sex Offenders and the Criminal Justice System*. London: Routledge.

Schroeder, K. C. (2002) 'Discourses of fact', in K. Bruhn Jensen (ed.) *A Handbook of Media and Communication Research: Qualitative and Quantitative Methodologies*. London: Routledge.

Sekula, A. (1982) 'On the invention of photographic meaning', in V. Burgin (ed.) *Thinking Photography*. London: Macmillan.

Sekula, A. (1986) 'The body and the archive', *October*, 39, 3–64.

Seltzer, M. (1998) *Serial Killers: Death and Life in America's Wound Culture*. London: Routledge.

Sexual Offences Act 2003, available at http://web.lexis-nexis.com/professional.

Seymour-Smith, C. (1986) *Macmillan Dictionary of Anthropology*. London: Macmillan.

Seymour-Ure, C. (1977) 'National daily papers and the party system', in O. Boyd-Barrett, C. Seymour-Ure and J. Tunstall (eds) *Studies on the Press*. Royal Commission on the Press Working Paper No. 3. London: Her Majesty's Stationery Office.

Seymour-Ure, C. (1998) 'Are the broadsheets becoming unhinged?', in J. Seaton (ed.) *Politics and the Media: Harlots and Prerogatives at the Turn of the Millennium*. Oxford: Blackwell.

Silverman, J. and D. Wilson (2002) *Innocence Betrayed: Paedophilia, The Media and Society*. Cambridge: Polity.

Simmel, G. (1964) 'The metropolis and mental life', in K. H. Wolff (ed.) *The Sociology of Georg Simmel*. London: Macmillan.

Simmel, G. (1971) 'The stranger', in D. N. Levine (ed.) *On Individuality and Social Forms: Selected Writings of Georg Simmel*. Chicago: University of Chicago Press.

Simon-Vandenbergen, A. M. (1986) 'Aspects of style in British newspapers', *Studia Germanica Gandensia*, 9.

Sommerville, C. J. (1982) *The Rise and Fall of Childhood*. London: Sage.

Sontag, S. (1979) *On Photography*. Harmondsworth: Penguin.

Stainton Rogers, W. and R. Stainton Rogers (1992) *Stories of Childhood*. London: Harvester Wheatsheaf.

Steedman, C. (1990) *Childhood, Culture and Class in Britain: Margaret McMillan, 1860–1931*. London: Virago.

Sztompka, P. (1999) *Trust: A Sociological Theory*. Cambridge: Cambridge University Press.

Taylor, M. and E. Quayle (2003) *Child Pornography: An Internet Crime*. Hove: Brunner-Routledge.

Thomas, T. (2000) *Sex Crime: Sex Offending and Society*. Cullompton: Willan.

Thompson, K. (1992) *Moral Panics*. London: Routledge.

Travis, A. (3 October 2002) 'Blunkett to raise police numbers by 2500', *Guardian*, p. 8.

Travis, A. (20 November 2002) 'Overhaul of ancient legislation widely welcome', *Guardian*, p. 4.

Travis, A. (8 May 2003) 'Blunkett to bypass judges on life sentences', *Guardian*, p. 6.

Tunstall, J. (1996) *Newspaper Power: The New National Press in Britain*. Oxford: Clarendon Press.

Ungar, S. (2001) 'Moral panic versus the risk society: the implications of the changing sites of social anxiety', *British Journal of Sociology*, 52:2, 271–91.

Valentine, G. (1996) 'Angels and devils: moral landscapes of childhood', *Environment and Planning D: Society and Space*, 14, 581–99.

Valentine, G. (2001) *Social Geographies: Space and Society*. London: Prentice Hall.

Valentine, G. and S. L. Holloway (2001) 'On-line dangers? Geographies of parents' fear for children's safety in cyberspace', *Professional Geographer*, 53:1, 71–83.

Valentine, G. and J. McKendrick (1997) 'Children's outdoor play: exploring parental concerns about children's safety and the changing nature of childhood', *Geoforum*, 28:2, 219–35.

Valentine, G., S. L. Holloway and N. Bingham (2000) 'Transforming cyberspace: children's interventions in the new public sphere', in S. L. Holloway and G. Valentine (eds) *Children's Geographies: Playing, Living, Learning*. London: Routledge.

Valier, C. (2002) *Theories of Crime and Punishment*. Harlow: Longman.

Van Dijk, T. A. (1993) 'Stories and racism', in D. K. Mumby (ed.) *Narrative and Social Control: Critical Perspectives*. London: Sage.

Van Loon, J. (2000) 'Virtual risks in the age of cybernetic reproduction', in B. Adam, U. Beck and J. Van Loon (eds) *The Risk Society and Beyond: Critical Issues for Social Theory*. London: Sage.

Wainwright, M. and F. al Yafai (15 July 2003) 'Hunt for girl, 12, and US marine, 31, she met on the internet', *Guardian*, p. 3.

West, D. (1996) 'Sexual molesters', in N. Walker (ed.) *Dangerous People*. London: Blackstone Press.

Williamson, J. (1978) *Decoding Advertisements: Ideology and Meaning in Advertising*. London: Boyars.

Wilson, C. (13 January 2004) 'Seen and not heard', *Guardian*, p. 24.

Wyre, R. (1996) 'The mind of the paedophile', in P. Bibby (ed.) *Organised Abuse: The Current Debate*. Basingstoke: Arena.

Young, S. (2001) 'What's the big idea? Production, consumption and internet regulatory discourse', *Media International Australia*, 101, 9–18.

Zelizer, V. (1985) *Pricing the Priceless Child*. New York: Basic Books.

Index